U.S.News & World Report

STYLEBOOK
for Writers and Editors

*This Book was Donated to the
Grayson County Public Library
by
Dr. & Mrs. Frank F. Merker
of Troutdale*

STYLEBOOK
for Writers and Editors

Prepared by Turner Rose

and a committee of *USN&WR* editors:

John H. Adams, *Executive Editor*

Lester Tanzer, *Managing Editor*

David E. Pollard, *Chief, News Desk*

LeRoy Mattingly, *Production Editor*

Robert G. Smith, *General Editor*

Donald Becker, *Chief, Text Desk*

U.S.News & World Report, Inc., Washington, D.C.

This book was composed by the Data Communications Department
of *U.S.News & World Report* on an Atex 8000 system,
and typeset on a Videocomp 500.

Editorial reading by Marion Todaro.

Library of Congress Cataloging in Publication Data

Rose, Turner, 1910–
    U.S. news & world report stylebook.

    Includes bibliographical references and index.
    1. Journalism—Handbooks, manuals, etc.
I. Adams, John Hanly, 1918–   II, The United States
news & world report. III. Title. IV. Title: Stylebook.
PN4783.R6   651.7'402   77–21337
ISBN 0–89193–001–9

TO THE STAFF

The purpose of this new stylebook, which took more than a year to prepare, is to help tell the news clearly and accurately.

This book is based on today's needs and today's ways, but where necessary it retains traditional aids to precise writing and easy reading. It also promotes a measure of uniformity that is important if ours is to appear before the public as a careful, authoritative magazine.

What we have here is an essential tool. I urge you to use it.

MARVIN L. STONE, Editor
U.S. News & World Report

WHY A STYLEBOOK

We write the news to inform; to tell people what is going on, so that they can judge for themselves how to further their own interests, how to fulfill their obligations to society and how to take intelligent part in running their country.

In these days of great events that affect individual lives, the news is acutely important to people. But surveys show that competing activities put a tight squeeze on time for reading. Therefore the magazine that serves readers best is the one that tells them what they want to know, and does it with the least waste of their effort. This service calls for a simple, direct, free-flowing and contemporary style.

Such a style transmits a feel of being on the scene. It uses the rich resources of popular speech, yet it keeps a hold on clarity: In employing new words and combinations, it must make sure that they are familiar to all groups and in all regions—or that they are explained by the context or the writer.

A good style also spells its words in a uniform way and constructs its sentences in recognizable forms, because this indicates that writers and editors know what they are doing and thus gives their product the ring of authenticity. A good style avoids vague statements, tangled language and all other blunders that delay or mislead.

Those are some of the reasons why we need a stylebook.

TURNER ROSE

HOW TO USE THIS BOOK

The *USN&WR* manual of style has two main parts: a series of organized chapters and a detailed, alphabetized index. To get the best results from them:

Consult the index. The combined Index and Word List is designed to answer most of your questions on the spot. In addition to capsuled rules, it displays the chosen spellings of a few hundred words. These spellings are cited because a choice was forced by disagreement among dictionaries, or because they were the forms judged most in keeping with *U.S.News & World Report* style, or because the words have been often misspelled or questioned.

Follow the paragraph references. Not every question of grammar and style can be answered in a half-dozen words. For that reason many index references offer paragraph and page references to the organized chapters. Even where an answer is given in the index, it may be useful to see further explanation and examples, or the body of guides into which the particular rule is fitted.

Suppose you can't find a rule or item because you don't know the name of it—for example, what to call a Mormon official? Find Mormon in the index, then consult the section in the main body of the book.

Or study the chapters. Consult the Table of Contents at the beginning of the book to find the desired chapter and section.

Make additions and notes as needed. Space has been provided at the ends of chapters and between the items of the word list.

TABLE OF CONTENTS

CAPITALIZATION

PUNCTUATION

FIGURES

FOREIGN CURRENCIES

NAMES OF PERSONS

NATIVES, NATIONALS

CHURCH AND CLERGY

WEAPONS, PLANES, ASTRONAUTICS

MEDICAL TERMS

TRADEMARKS

POLITICAL REGIONS OF THE U.S.

CAPTIONS, CHARTS, BOXES, CREDITS

SLANG, DIALECT, JARGON

COMPOUND WORDS

INDEX AND WORD LIST

STYLE AND CONTENT

Anatomy of Style

1.0 Our objective is a fast-moving, informative flow of words, one that also holds people's attention.

1.1 A mixture of short and longer sentences, with a variety of constructions, will help to keep the reader alert and interested. Sudden insertion of a short, blunt sentence achieves emphasis. No sentence should be so long that the reader loses track of the beginning before he comes to the end; re-examination of an article frequently turns up a sentence or two of this kind.

1.2 A succession of one-sentence paragraphs, favored by some writers, does not necessarily help clarity; it may have the opposite effect because the reader is left to puzzle out what is related to what and how. Newsmagazine paragraphs should be reasonably short, it is true, but with each paragraph organized around a topic. An exception is a collection of single-sentence paragraphs in a series introduced by a colon or a dash.

Logic in Series

1.3 Below the sentence level, a series must consist of parallel constructions if it is to be logical and readable.

> BAD: Drinking late at night can cause belligerency, exhaustion, indigestion and increase absenteeism.
>
> CORRECT: Drinking late at night can cause belligerency, exhaustion and indigestion and increase absenteeism.
>
> BETTER: Drinking late at night can cause belligerency, exhaustion and indigestion. It also increases absenteeism.
>
> BAD: Mr. Jones cited three reasons for buying municipal bonds:
>
> • Long-run stability
>
> • Tax-free status
>
> • They give the holder a stake in the community.

Two of these points are things, the third is a statement. They do not fit together in a package and therefore the combination is harder to read.

Multiple Adjectives

1.4   We are all right with "big threshing machine" or "young, happy people," but many strings of modifiers are confusing or obstructive to the reader. The classic case is "pink lady's pocketbook." Here is an example:

> Now farmers are planting from fence to fence to meet soaring world food demand and the search is on . . .

Of course the writer knew in advance exactly what he meant to say, so the result seemed fine to him. But as readers we are forced into an unnecessary exercise. First we see "soaring world." Reject that, it doesn't fit. Then, "soaring world food." Are we talking about soaring food? No. So finally we come to "demand" and apply all the modifiers to it.

Granted that the skillful reader can cope with this, why make him do it? We can easily write, ". . . the world's soaring demand for food . . ." and put the modifiers next to the words they modify.

Mixed Metaphors

1.5   Garbled figures of speech are illogical at best, ridiculous at worst.

> BAD: The agency is on the horns of a dilemma, whichever way the cat jumps.

Overdrawn? This came in a piece of copy submitted for publication.

Exact Words vs. Inexact

1.6   Writing serves the reader better if the writer defines his terms, at least to himself. What is "upper class"? (We're not supposed to have one in America.) What is "middle class"? What is "Northeast"? If we know what we mean, we can get closer to the facts. In the search for exact terms it's useful to avoid, so far as possible, some words that are cop-outs. Examples:

At Columbus, Ohio, a new *facility* for the Nessel Company is nearing completion.

What is it? A bathroom? A 3-acre factory?

In Denver, a new library is *under way*.

Is somebody campaigning for a new library? Are plans being drawn for . . . ? Has ground been broken for . . . ? Is work nearly complete on . . . ? Is the library already in operation?

Many villages have given up their local jails.

It would add a lot to our credibility if we could say, "More than 300 villages in the U.S. have given up their local jails."

Who Said It?

1.7

Officials said . . .
Observers said . . .
Experts said . . .
A spokesman said . . .

These phrases are evasive; they can leave the general reader vaguely unsatisfied and the insider suspecting that the officials are a doorman, the observers are a bartender, the experts are our reporter and the spokesman is the third vice president's secretary. What we have to do is get as close as possible to naming real persons, so that we will seem to know what we are talking about. Sample lines of retreat—

For *officials*:

Secretary of Agriculture Franklin Farman

a top official in the Department of Agriculture

officials who have studied the agreement

Agriculture officials

federal officials or officials in Washington

For *observers*:

British Ambassador Hilary John

a Western ambassador who is a veteran in the Middle Eastern service

a veteran diplomat

Western diplomats on the scene

old hands in the Middle East

Quotations

1.8   We use two main kinds of quotations: (1) language in or from printed articles, documents, letters and similar records, including *USN&WR* interviews that have been reviewed and approved by the interviewees; (2) language attributed to others in reporters' memories or notes. These two kinds require a shade of difference in treatment, outlined below.

1.9   **When language is on record,** we have no call to make any changes beyond those required by printing style, such as spelling words our way or moving commas from a position after quotation marks to before—and even here, we have to be careful if there is a danger of altering the meaning. If we leave anything out, we must indicate a deletion. To condense or otherwise change a statement so that it sounds better in our context—unless we have the writer's permission—is beyond our province; the only way to make such changes is to paraphrase, outside of quotation marks.

1.10   **In quotations from memory** or from notes taken on the scene, it is up to a reporter to tell what the person said, not what he thinks the person meant to say or ought to have said. If the quote does not make sense as spoken, the only solutions are to give up the quote or query the person quoted. Details such as punctuation are naturally the duty of the reporter and the editors, who must put in the commas and periods in such a way as to give the most accurate rendition of what was spoken.

1.11   **Pronunciation** is largely in the ear of the hearer. It is hard to prove how somebody spoke, and, in any case, doubt always remains as to whose pronunciation is right. To call attention to pronunciation by misspelling a word is often to ridicule the speaker. A large newspaper caused an uproar by quoting a man as saying "Nigra." Only in a rare case—for instance, in an article about a member of Congress who makes a point of being a personality or when we know it is all right with the person quoted—should we ever stress pronunciation.

1.12   **A quotee's grammar** is his own and should not routinely be cleaned up to meet our own publishing standards. Even a college professor should not be made to talk as if he or she were lecturing. If the professor told us, "I don't know who we ought to hire," we should let him say it that way. On the other hand, if he said, "Them boys . . ." and we don't think he said it on purpose, we may judge it best to change it and spare him embarrassment.

(For typographical treatment of quotations, see 5.35 to 5.48.)

Slang

1.13   See Chapter 16.

Profanity and Obscenity

1.14   Of course we don't write profane or obscene words of our own. The question boils down to which words of others we should quote and when we should quote them. A hell or damn doesn't bother many people when it seems necessary to an incident reported. If an official says, "Unemployment is damn bad here," we should quote him—but we had best make sure he said it. If he says, "Hell, I don't see any problem," the word is just dragged in and we needn't quote him unless we are trying to get across the impression that he is a loose talker. There is also the problem that if the local preacher gets after him he may say we misquoted him.

We no longer have to think up a substitute for a matter-of-fact word like *rape. SOB* is acceptable for *son of a bitch.*

When we go further, however, we are on shaky ground. More-strenuous curse words and obscenities will have to be very necessary to the story in order to be worth the trouble they get us into. There are occasions when quotation is worth it: As the *New York Times* points out, in the case of the true Watergate tapes the whole thing had to be given to the public, dirty words and all. These cases do occur, but the writer or desk editor can't take the responsibility on his own. Top editors must be consulted.

1.15   When a top editor has decided to omit an obscenity or a profane expression from a statement that is on record in print or by TV or radio or is common knowledge in any other way, we have to make clear that something is left out. This is done by use of three asterisks:

"I don't care if the * * * can type," he said.

If the profanity or obscenity occurred in a statement made to one of our own writers or reporters, and if a decision is made not to use the word or words, it may be cleaned up judiciously—with care not to distort the meaning:

"I don't care if she can type," he said.

Fairness

1.16 Extreme care is required in dealing with criminal charges, court suits and other accusations.

1.17 **Factual correctness** is the first, though not the only, consideration. Newspaper clips and wire-service items are not enough backup when crime or misbehavior is concerned. We have to get as close as possible to official sources. Quoting a person or publication does not excuse us for a mistake of fact or judgment, even though in some cases we can show better faith by attributing a statement than by making it on our own.

1.18 **Up-to-date information** is essential. It is unsafe to write without checking the possibility of appeal, new evidence or other change. Therefore we must keep contact with the situation, never work just from old material.

1.19 **Both sides** are important. If a person is accused in any manner or his position is attacked, every effort must be made to present his reply. If our sources have not provided any response, it is up to us to look for one.

1.20 **Suitable words** are a matter for careful choice and examination, to avoid any implication of guilt when guilt has not been proved in court. "Arrested for theft" is the classic error of this type. "Arrested on a charge of theft" is one right way to say it if that really is the charge—and we had best make certain it is an official charge. Other references have to be watched at least as closely. *The culprits* and similar phrases make trouble on two counts. First, they lump together several individuals, some of whom may suffer by association. Second, they may indicate guilt when no guilt has been proved.

1.21 **Allegations** of bad behavior by a public official may be subject to restriction unless they concern the administration of office. Doubt has been cast on the defense that social prominence opens the way to damaging news. And the excuse that a mistake was made without malice has been turned down by courts.

1.22 **Caption writing** presents a special risk. Crowd scenes in which people can be identified are often troublesome; for instance, if a photograph illustrates a crime or disorder, our description must be tailored to avoid implicating any persons who might be innocent bystanders. A child's face in a story about classes for the retarded must be treated with the utmost caution: If he is not retarded, we of course get into serious trouble by leaving any implication that he might be; but even if he is, we might have to worry about causing pain or embarrassment. The Art Section is responsible for getting releases signed for photographs, but we have to make sure captions and contexts do not go beyond the purposes understood by the signers.

1.23 **Legal advice** is important. All statements concerning arrests, charges and rulings or raising questions of libel or invasion of privacy should be examined by legal experts on our own staff, and in cases of heavy legal content the management will arrange to send copy to a consultant.

Keeping Current

1.24 The need to take note of the latest, in large concerns or small, goes beyond legal cases. The problem is not only that a case may have been dismissed, deferred or appealed. Bills in a state legislature may have been passed or defeated, lost people may have been found, feuding politicians may have made up, local prices may have risen, building projects may have been abandoned. And even if our story was correct when written yesterday, something may have happened since. Both the writer and the editor should spot those things that could change, and keep watch over them till publication. This principle is elementary, but it sometimes is forgotten.

Language That Fits

1.25 Words and parts of sentences sometimes are forced into molds where they will not fit. Examples from submitted copy:

> The third base at Northwest Cape, x x x

There were not three bases at Northwest Cape. The writer meant:

> The third base, at Northwest Cape, x x x

Again:

> x x x before former President Nixon arrived in Moscow x x x

Nixon was President when he arrived in Moscow, although he was former President at the time of writing. It might have been said this way:

> x x x before the Moscow arrival of Richard Nixon, who then was President x x x

Or, if the context was clear, he might have been referred to simply as President Nixon.

And again:

> x x x officials negotiating a new Pine Gap accord—which expires December 9—still insist x x x

The new Pine Gap accord was not to expire December 9, but that is what the sentence says. It should be:

> x x x officials negotiating a successor to the present Pine Gap accord—which expires December 9—still insist x x x

Word Origins

1.26   Words from classical languages frequently are misspelled; confusion of singular and plural is widespread. Some dictionaries have come to sanction several erroneous usages simply because the dictionary way is to record whatever anybody is doing. But misuse through plain ignorance is not the kind of change that improves or enriches. On the contrary: Respect for the origins and principles of language can keep it workable.

Examples—

> *an agenda:* ACCEPTABLE. This is strictly a plural, but usage to mean a program for action has become so deeply embedded in the language that it cannot be ruled out.
>
> *a bacteria:* WRONG, though incredibly popping up in copy. What the writer may mean is a genus, species or strain of bacteria (see 12.3). Usually the correct singular, *a bacterium,* would do just as well.
>
> *a criteria:* WRONG. The singular is *criterion.*
>
> *this data:* TO BE AVOIDED. *Data* is a plural word meaning pieces of information, and the correct expression, both grammatically and logically, is *these data.* Sometimes *data* amounts to jargon and should give way to a common word like *information.*

an insignia: WRONG. If you don't like "an insigne," call it a symbol, emblem, badge, shoulder patch, shield, whatever it is.

1.27   *Magna Charta, Magna Carta:* BOTH CORRECT, but our spelling is Charta because that is the spelling preferred by all major dictionaries including the Oxford English. We could spare ourselves a lot of unnecessary arguments by considering where *Charta* came from. The root word is Greek and starts with the letter *chi,* which is pronounced to sound like a *k* far back in the throat. The Romans, having no single letter to produce this sound, spelled it *ch* to put the breath in it. We no longer pronounce it that way and could drop the *h*—but time enough for that when *Christ* is spelled *Crist.*

It's O.K. to Have a—

1.28   **Preposition at end of sentence.** It's better than an awkward phrase. That applies in headlines, too.

1.29   **Split infinitive.** Often clearer and cleaner than an attempt to avoid it. Use it when needed.

General Cautions

1.30   **In precedes to texts and interviews,** avoid any suggestion that the material has been edited. Don't speak of a "condensation," for instance, but say, "Following are excerpts . . ." or "The foregoing is from an address by . . ." or "What follows is the full text of a section of the report. . . ." Include the name of the person being interviewed in the first question of an interview.

1.31   **In precedes to datelined articles,** do not refer to the locale as "here." The dateline does not cover the precede, which is written in the editorial offices in Washington.

1.32   **Hedging for possible breaks** in the news is important. Make sure that we will not sound silly because of something that happens over the weekend. This requires special attention to tenses and qualifying phrases.

1.33   **When a section is introduced by a colon,** the section must be marked in some way to distinguish it from subsequent matter that does not depend on the colon. Ways to do this include:

numbering the paragraphs, starting the paragraphs with 4-point bullets, using a sidehead to introduce the new topic that follows the colon-based material, using a transitional phrase.

1.34 **Telegraphese** often looks amateurish. Do not make a general practice of dropping *the, a* and *an* from copy.

1.35 **Unwanted read-ins** may occur when an abbreviation at the end of a sentence seems to read into the next sentence. For example: "This situation was worse in the U.S. Government sources reported an unfavorable trade balance." This example can be cured by spelling out *United States.* In other cases the parts of the first sentence may be shifted or the beginning of the second sentence changed. Such changes cannot be made in a text, of course. If made in an interview, they are subject to approval by the interviewee.

1.36 **Undue repetition of words and phrases** is boring and unpleasant. Do not sprinkle the copy with "now" and "new." Look for appropriate synonyms. Watch out for phrases that are likely to run through the magazine in story after story, such as "more and more," "questions are being raised," "all across the country," "at the same time." Use these where they are really needed, but do not drag them in.

Spelling

1.37 Words in *USN&WR* are spelled according to these guides:

1. The word list at the end of this book.

2. For words not in the list, Webster's New World Dictionary, published by Collins-World.

3. For words not in the list or the New World Dictionary, Webster's Third New International Dictionary, published by G. & C. Merriam Company.

Webster's New Collegiate Dictionary, 1973 and after, is the basis for word division at the ends of lines.

Geographic Names

1.38 Except where otherwise noted in this manual, geographic names will be spelled as in the *Columbia Lippincott Gazetteer of the World.* Though outdated, Columbia Lippincott still is the only comprehensive and generally satisfactory guide. Individual names should be modernized by agreement as seems advisable and entered in the manual. For names not in other sources, consult the *National Geographic Atlas of the World.*

NOTES

BIAS: AVOID IT

2.0   Bias in news writing may be ethnic, national, racial, sectional, religious, sexual. All these biases have their origins in easy assumptions and a lack of consideration. Since much bias is subconscious, conscious effort is necessary to avoid it. Some lines to follow:

2.1   **Words.** It goes without saying that terms such as *spik, wop, Jap* and *Mick* are ruled out. *Redneck* and *hillbilly* should be shunned but sometimes are not. *Bible belt* is offensive both to Bible readers and to the nonreligious; don't say it unless you want to insult a whole section, whatever section that may be. Some blacks object to *Negro* but some utter it themselves; use must be judicious. *Colored* is banned except in reference to persons of mixed blood in Africa. *Chicano* is readily accepted by many groups with Mexican connections, but care is indicated in referring to individuals because a few may object.

2.2   **Concepts.** Do not make assumptions about whole nationalities, races or religions; many of these assumptions are offensive to some or all of the people involved. Don't imply that a group is typically belligerent, unwashed, ignorant, greedy, poverty-stricken, small-bodied, filthy rich, tricky, toothy, fond of greasy food, or afflicted with some other stereotyped trait.

2.3   **Associations.** Don't couple racial or ethnic names with undesirable conditions. For instance:

    Don't write about "a run-down Puerto Rican section"; the Puerto Ricans didn't run it down.

    Don't refer to a "black ghetto"; the basic meaning of *ghetto* is a place a given group is forbidden by law to leave, so the word is argumentative and gives the world an incorrect impression. Also, the phrase identifies blacks with degraded living.

    Don't use the sarcastic "WASP enclave" and similar phrases; they misrepresent the sentiments and style of a numerous group of Americans.

    These injunctions do not mean that the facts should be withheld when pertinent to a story. In an election article, for example, if it is important that a certain area is poor and that it is inhabited mostly by Puerto Ricans, tell things the way they are—but not in a close combination that sounds offensive.

2.4   **Accents.** Be careful about quoting what you regard as peculiarities of speech, especially by misspelling words; the primary implication is derogatory, and, besides, the trouble might be in your ear.

Problems of Sexism

2.5   Where you can do so without obscuring your meaning or making monsters of sentences, avoid words regarded as sexist. With ingenuity, this usually is possible.

Hardest to deal with is *he*, in the sense of *a certain person* or *that person*:

> If a person wants to travel abroad, he must have a passport.

The pronoun *one*, as a substitute here for *person* and *he*, often sounds awkward. It should be used sparingly.

He or she can sometimes be employed, but beware of repetition.

That leaves us rewriting. We can say:

> Persons traveling abroad must have passports.

> You can't travel abroad without a passport.

> For travel abroad, a passport is required.

Another example:

> A member of Congress is likely to regard the allowance for staff salaries as his personal property.

One possible substitute:

> A member of Congress is likely to regard the allowance for staff salaries as personal property.

A study of the collection that follows will provide an idea of the kinds of words often considered sexist. They are only examples. The substitutes also are only examples; they will not serve in every case, but they indicate how alternatives may be found.

Consider alternatives to language that identifies the male as the archetype of the human race. Substitutions need not always be made when the cure would be worse than the disease.

Words Objected To	Possible Substitutes
man, mankind	humankind, the human race, people
man's accomplishments	human accomplishments
the workingman	working people
the man for the job	the person for the job
man-made	synthetic, machine-made
the common man	ordinary people

Consider alternatives to language that implies certain occupations are in the exclusive domain of men or of women, that betrays surprise at finding a female in a profession or executive position, that emphasizes the person's sex.

businessmen	business people
businessman, businesswoman	business executive
mailman	mail carrier
councilman	council member
chairman	the chair, presiding officer
foreman	supervisor
eight-man board	eight-member board
woman lawyer, lady doctor	lawyer, doctor
poetess	poet
male nurse	nurse
housewife	homemaker
co-ed	student
career girl	(name the job or profession)

Avoid language that stereotypes women as sex objects, as cute, scatterbrained, timorous, shrewish.

a blonde	(just don't go into that)
cute	(don't go into that either)
pert	(and don't go into that)
all atwitter	excited
hesitating womanlike	proceeding carefully
shrewish	quick to retort
the fair sex	women
the distaff side	women, the women of the family
girls	women, if they're 18 or older
libber	feminist

NOTE: It's no longer "workmen's compensation." The government's official term is "workers' compensation."

NOTES

ABBREVIATIONS

Addresses

3.0 Spell out and capitalize *Street, Avenue, Place*, etc. when used as part of an address.

Clock Time

3.1 If immediately connected with figures, use *a.m.* and *p.m.* Use colon to separate hours and minutes.

  4:30 p.m.   5 a.m.

If clock time is expressed as daylight-saving time or standard time, the following abbreviations are used:

EST   CST   MST   PST
EDT   CDT   MDT   PDT

At 6 a.m. CST he left the hospital and drove home.

College Degrees

3.2 Abbreviate as follows:

  A.B. or B.A.—bachelor of arts

  B.S.—bachelor of science

  D.D.—doctor of divinity

  D.D.S.—doctor of dental surgery

  LL.D.—doctor of laws

  M.A.—master of arts

  M.D.—doctor of medicine

  Ph.D.—doctor of philosophy

NOTE: *USN&WR* policy is to reserve the title "Dr." for medical doctors, dentists.

Company Names

3.3   Spell out and capitalize *Company, Corporation, Railroad, Railway, Brothers* as parts of company names when they appear in the body of an article.

Abbreviate *Inc.* and *Ltd.* and separate from rest of name with comma. Also use comma after if sentence continues:

> Happy Times, Inc., offers a three-week tour.

Inc. and *Ltd.* are not necessary if *Company, Corporation, Railroad, Railway, Sons* or other language clearly indicating a company name is used. BUT: Frelinghuysen Chairbottoms, Inc.; Jesse Filbert, Ltd.

Abbreviations *Co., Corp., Bro., Bros., R.R., Ry.* may be used in charts, boxes, maps. In a tight squeeze, *Co.* or *Corp.* may be left out.

Company and *Corporation* are not always necessary in running copy if the name is familiar and the context is clear. *Ford Motor, General Motors* and *General Electric* are good enough in most places; *Brown & Williamson* often will do in a story about tobacco.

Use *&* in all names of business and legal firms; use *and* in governmental units, unions, trade or professional groups.

Where the full name of a railroad ends with *Company,* this word is omitted.

Where *GmbH, AG, OHG* or *KG* is affixed to the name of a German firm, use the abbreviation without a comma. The same rule applies to *SA* in names of French or Spanish firms.

> EXAMPLES OF NAMES: Ford Motor Company, General Motors Corporation, Union Pacific Railroad, Long Island Rail Road, Grenville Castings, Ltd., Food and Drug Administration, Boot and Shoe Workers Union, Brown Brothers Harriman & Company, Brown & Williamson Tobacco Corporation, Gummiwerke Fulda GmbH, Daimler-Benz AG

Where a company's name is to be abbreviated with initials on subsequent reference, omit periods unless they are part of the official name:

> Johnson Rotary Pump Company; JRP
>
> J.R.P. Company; J.R.P.

Compass Directions

3.4 Directions should be spelled out in running copy except in street addresses. In maps, charts, etc. they may be abbreviated: *E, W, SE, NNW.*

Geographic Names

3.5 **States, territories.** Abbreviate states and territories after the name of a city or other geographical term or, if necessary, when used in tables, maps or charts.

Following are abbreviations for states:

Alabama—Ala.	Montana—Mont.
Alaska—spell out	Nebraska—Nebr.
Arizona—Ariz.	Nevada—Nev.
Arkansas—Ark.	New Hampshire—N.H.
California—Calif.	New Jersey—N.J.
Colorado—Colo.	New Mexico—N.M.
Connecticut—Conn.	New York—N.Y.
Delaware—Del.	North Carolina—N.C.
District of Columbia—D.C.	North Dakota—N.D.
Florida—Fla.	Ohio—spell out
Georgia—Ga.	Oklahoma—Okla.
Hawaii—spell out	Oregon—Oreg.
Idaho—spell out	Pennsylvania—Pa.
Illinois—Ill.	Rhode Island—R.I.
Indiana—Ind.	South Carolina—S.C.
Iowa—spell out	South Dakota—S.D.
Kansas—Kans.	Tennessee—Tenn.
Kentucky—Ky.	Texas—Tex.
Louisiana—La.	Utah—spell out
Maine—Me.	Vermont—Vt.
Maryland—Md.	Virginia—Va.
Massachusetts—Mass.	Washington—Wash.
Michigan—Mich.	West Virginia—W.Va.
Minnesota—Minn.	Wisconsin—Wis.
Mississippi—Miss.	Wyoming—Wyo.
Missouri—Mo.	

In a very tight spot on a map or chart, *Ida.* and *Ia.* may be used.

Other geographical divisions that are under U.S. jurisdiction:

Canal Zone—C.Z.	Samoa—spell out
Guam—spell out	Virgin Islands—V.I.
Puerto Rico—P.R.	

3.6   **Canadian provinces** and territories:

Alberta—Alta.	Northwest Territories—N.W.T.
British Columbia—B.C.	Nova Scotia—N.S.
Labrador (part of New- foundland)—Lab.	Ontario—Ont.
	Prince Edward Island—P.E.I.
Manitoba—Man.	Quebec—Que.
Newfoundland—Nfld.	Saskatchewan—Sask.
New Brunswick—N.B.	

(For words denoting natives or residents of the provinces, see 9.1.)

3.7   **Saint, Sainte, Fort, Mount.** In geographical names, use the abbreviations *St.* and *Ste.*
EXCEPTION: Spell out Saint John, N.B., which does not like to be mistaken for St. John's, Nfld. Do the same for any other city with a similar story.

Spell out *Fort* in names of cities and Army posts.

Spell out *Mount* in names of cities and mountains.

3.8   **Names of Countries.** The following forms may be used in charts, boxes and maps, but spell out the names whenever possible. For convenience, some lands that are not national entities have been included in this list.

Afghanistan—Afgh.

Albania—Alb.

American Samoa—Amer. Sam.

Andorra—And.

Angola—Ang.

Argentina—Arg.

Australia—Austral.

Austria—Aust.

Bahamas—Bah.

Bahrain—Bahr.

Bangladesh—Bangla.; Bngl.; Bd.

Barbados—Barb.

Belgium—Belg.

Benin—Benin

Bhutan—Bhu.

Bolivia—Bol.

Botswana—Botswana

Brazil—Braz.

British Virgin Islands—Br. Vir. Is.

Bulgaria—Bulg.

Burma—Bur.

Burundi—Burundi

Cambodia—Camb.

Cameroon—Cam.

Canada—Can.

Central African Empire—Cen. Af. Emp.

Ceylon—see Sri Lanka

Chad—Chad

Chile—Chile

China (People's Republic of)—China

Congo (People's Republic of,
   formerly Congo-Brazzaville)—Congo

Costa Rica—C.R.

Cuba—Cuba

Cyprus—Cyprus

Czechoslovakia—Czech.

Denmark—Den.

Djibouti—Djib.

Dominican Republic—Dom. Rep.

Ecuador—Ecua.

Egypt—Egypt

El Salvador—El Salv.

Equatorial Guinea—Eq. Guin.

Ethiopia—Eth.

Fiji—Fiji

Finland—Fin.

France—France

Gabon—Gabon

Gambia—Gam.

Germany

  East Germany—E. Germ.

  West Germany—W. Germ.

Ghana—Ghana

Great Britain—Britain, G.B.

Greece—Gr.

Grenada—Grenada

Guatemala—Guat.

Guinea—Guinea

Guinea-Bissau—Guin.-Biss.

Guyana—Guyana

Haiti—Haiti

Honduras—Hond.

Hungary—Hung.

Iceland—Ice.

India—India

Indonesia—Indon.

Iran—Iran

Iraq—Iraq

Ireland—Ire.

Israel—Israel

Italy—It.

Ivory Coast—Iv. Coast; I.C.

Jamaica—Jam.

Japan—Jap.

Jordan—Jor.

Kashmir—Kashmir

Kenya—Ken.

Korea—Kor.

Kuwait—Kuw.

Laos—Laos

Lebanon—Leb.

Lesotho—Lesotho

Liberia—Liberia

Libya—Lib.

Liechtenstein—Liecht.; Liech.

Luxembourg—Lux.

Madagascar—Madag.

Malawi—Malawi

Malaysia—Malay.; Mal.

Maldives—Mald.

Mali—Mali

Malta—Malta

Mauritania—Mauritania

Mauritius—Mauritius

Mexico—Mex.

Monaco—Mon.

Mongolia (do not use Mongolian People's Republic)—Mong.

Morocco—Mor.

Mozambique—Moz.

Namibia—Nam.

Nauru—Nauru

Nepal—Nepal

Netherlands—Neth.

New Zealand—N.Z.

Newfoundland—Nfld.

Nicaragua—Nicar.

Niger—Niger

Nigeria—Nigeria

Norway—Nor.

Oman—Oman

Pakistan—Pak.

Panama—Pan.

Papua New Guinea—Pap. N. Gn.

Paraguay—Para.

Peru—Peru

Philippines—Phil.

Poland—Pol.

Portugal—Port.

Puerto Rico—Puerto R.; P.R.

Qatar—Qatar

Reunion (no acute)—Reunion

Rhodesia—Rhod.

Río Muni—Río Muni

Rumania—Rum.

Rwanda—Rwanda

San Marino—S. Mar.

São Tomé and Príncipe—São Tomé Prin.; S. Tm. Prn.

Saudi Arabia—Saudi Ar.; Sau. Ar.

Scotland—Scot.

Senegal—Senegal

Seychelles—Seych.

Sierra Leone—Sa. Leone

Singapore—Singapore

Somalia—Som.

South Africa—S. Af.

Spain—Sp.

Spanish Sahara (see Western Sahara)

Sri Lanka—Sri Lanka

Sudan—Sud.

Suriname—Sur.

Swaziland—Swazi.; Swaz.

Sweden—Sw.

Switzerland—Switz.

Syria—Syr.

Taiwan—Taiwan

Tanzania—Tanz.; Tan.

Thailand—Thai.

Togo—Togo

Tonga—Tonga

Transkei—Trans.

Trinidad and Tobago—Trin. & Tob.

Tunisia—Tun.

Turkey—Turk.

Uganda—Uga.; Ug.

Union of Soviet Socialist Republics—U.S.S.R.

United Arab Emirates—U. Ar. Emr.

Upper Volta—Upper Volta

Uruguay—Uru.

Venezuela—Venez.

Vietnam, Socialist Republic of—Viet.

Wales—Wales

Western Sahara (interim name for former Spanish Sahara)—W. Sahara

Western Samoa—W. Samoa

Yemen, North—N. Yemen

Yemen, South—S. Yemen

Yugoslavia—Yug.

Zaire (no umlaut)—Zaire

Zambia—Zambia

Zimbabwe—Zimbabwe

(For nationalities and adjective forms of country names, see 9.2.)

Month, Year

3.9   Abbreviate month when used with date and year. In running copy, do not abbreviate the month when standing alone or when used with the year only or the day only. Abbreviations, or initial letters where clear in meaning, may be used in charts, boxes and maps.

January—Jan.	July—spell out
February—Feb.	August—Aug.
March—spell out	September—Sept.
April—spell out	October—Oct.
May—spell out	November—Nov.
June—spell out	December—Dec.

On Aug. 4, 1976, a celebration x x x

The meeting is scheduled for September 6.

After January, 1977, the law x x x

Abbreviate *Anno Domini* and *Before Christ* when with years, and use periods. A.D. should precede the year; B.C. should follow: A.D. 367; 2000 B.C.

Organizations, Agencies

3.10   Agencies and organizations commonly referred to by the abbreviation may be so treated in print. In most cases, the full name should be used on first reference in an article, before abbreviation is employed. AFL-CIO is an exception. In a tight lead, FBI and NATO may be abbreviated, but they then should be spelled out at the first good opportunity. Usually, abbreviations of agencies are formed from initials and are used without periods, but some of them need periods to avoid ambiguity or satisfy accepted usage.

(For treatment of companies, see 3.3, "Company Names.")

Examples:

AFL-CIO	American Federation of Labor–Congress of Industrial Organizations
COPE	AFL-CIO Committee on Political Education
CORE	Congress of Racial Equality
EEC	European Economic Community (Common Market)
EEOC	Equal Employment Opportunity Commission
ECOSOC	Economic and Social Council
ERDA	Energy Research and Development Administration
FAO	Food and Agriculture Organization
FBI	Federal Bureau of Investigation
FCC	Federal Communications Commission
FRB	Federal Reserve Board
GATT	General Agreement on Tariffs and Trade
GNMA	Government National Mortgage Association
HUD	Department of Housing and Urban Development
IMF	International Monetary Fund
NAACP	National Association for the Advancement of Colored People
NATO	North Atlantic Treaty Organization
NLRB	National Labor Relations Board
OECD	Organization for Economic Cooperation and Development
OPEC	Organization of Petroleum Exporting Countries

OPIC	Overseas Private Investment Corporation
OSHA	Occupational Safety and Health Administration
RAF	Royal Air Force
RN	Royal Navy
ROTC	Reserve Officers' Training Corps
SEC	Securities and Exchange Commission
SHAPE	Supreme Headquarters, Allied Powers, Europe (NATO)
UMW	United Mine Workers of America
U.N.	United Nations
UNESCO	United Nations Educational, Scientific and Cultural Organization
U.S.	United States
USA	United States Army (in military titles)
USAF	United States Air Force (in military titles)
USCG	United States Coast Guard (in military titles)
USMC	United States Marine Corps (in military titles)
USN	United States Navy (in military titles)
U.S.S.R.	Union of Soviet Socialist Republics
USN&WR	*U.S.News & World Report* (in charts, credits; may be abbreviated in running copy after first reference)
VA	Veterans Administration
WHO	World Health Organization

Sovereigns

3.11   Names of sovereigns are expressed in the following manner, no periods or commas being used after or before Roman numeral:

Elizabeth II   Pope Paul VI

Titles

3.12   Civil and military titles listed here should be abbreviated when used before full name (but note exceptions), spelled out before surname only. They also should be spelled out when used without names: The governor, a doctor, an admiral, the general. (For capitalization of titles, see 4.40-4.45.)

3.13   **Civil titles.** Abbreviate as follows:

Attorney General—Atty. Gen.

Doctor—Dr. (for physicians and dentists only)

Governor—Gov. (abbreviate only in a series, chart, box or map)

Lieutenant Governor—Lt. Gov.

Honorable—Hon.

Member of Parliament—M.P. (military police, MP)

Professor—Prof.

Representative—Rep. (abbreviate only in a series, chart, box or map): Otherwise, Representative Gawin Swanson (D-Va.)

Reverend—Rev.

Right Honorable—Rt. Hon.

Right Reverend—Rt. Rev.

Senator—Sen. (abbreviate only in a series, chart, box or map): Otherwise, Senator Anson Bruno (R-Wis.)

Very Reverend—Very Rev.

Superintendent—Supt. (abbreviate only in a series, chart, box or map)

3.14   **Military titles.** Abbreviations shown here are used as indicated with names. If necessary for space reasons, they may also be used in charts and tabular matter matching ranks with pay or other information. Military titles may be dropped on subsequent mention of a person by surname only, but frequently it is useful to keep them. In all cases, it is O.K. to use the last name without a title on subsequent mention.

(commissioned officers)

Army, Marine Corps, Air Force

Name of Rank	Before Full Name	Before Last Name (subsequent mention)	In Later Mention
General	Gen.	General	the general
Lieutenant General	Lt. Gen.	General	the general
Major General	Maj. Gen.	General	the general
Brigadier General	Brig. Gen.	General	the general
Colonel	Col.	Colonel	the colonel
Lieutenant Colonel	Lt. Col.	Colonel	the colonel
Major	Maj.	Major	the major
Captain	Capt.	Captain	the captain
First Lieutenant	1st Lt.	Lieutenant	the lieutenant
Second Lieutenant	2nd Lt.	Lieutenant	the lieutenant

Navy

Name of Rank	Before Full Name	Before Last Name (subsequent mention)	In Later Mention
Admiral	Adm.	Admiral	the admiral
Vice Admiral	Vice Adm.	Admiral	the admiral
Rear Admiral	Rear Adm.	Admiral	the admiral
Captain	Capt.	Captain	the captain
Commander	Cmdr.	Commander	the commander
Lieutenant Commander	Lt. Cmdr.	Commander	the commander
Lieutenant	Lt.	Lieutenant	the lieutenant
Lieutenant (junior grade)	Lt. (j.g.)	Lieutenant	the lieutenant
Ensign	Ens.	Ensign	the ensign

EXAMPLES:

Maj. Gen. Jesse Filbert; General Filbert; the general

Lt. Col. Xavier Filbert; Colonel Filbert; the colonel

Vice Adm. Max Filbert; Admiral Filbert; the admiral

Lt. (j.g.) Tom Filbert; Lieutenant Filbert; the lieutenant

(warrant officers)

All the services have warrant officers. Use the following:

Before Full Name	Before Last Name Only
Chief Warrant Officer	CWO
Warrant Officer	WO

EXAMPLE: Chief Warrant Officer Warren Brown; CWO Brown; the warrant officer

(enlisted ratings)

Army

Sergeant major of the Army should follow the name: Charles MacDowell, sergeant major of the Army; Sergeant MacDowell; the sergeant.

Before Full Name	Before Last Name Only
Command Sgt. Major	Sergeant
Staff Sgt. Maj.	Sergeant
1st Sgt.	Sergeant

Before Full Name	Before Last Name Only
Master Sgt.	Sergeant
Platoon Sgt.	Sergeant
Sgt. 1st Class	Sergeant
Specialist 7	Specialist
Staff Sgt.	Sergeant
Specialist 6	Specialist
Sgt.	Sergeant
Specialist 5	Specialist
Cpl.	Corporal
Specialist 4	Specialist
Pfc.	Private
Pvt.	Private

EXAMPLE: Command Sgt. Maj. Perry Sassoon; Sergeant Sassoon; the sergeant

Marine Corps

Names of ranks in the Marine Corps follow the Army model and should be treated in the same way, although the named ranks do not always correspond.

Two exceptions:

Master Gunnery Sgt.	Sergeant
Lance Cpl.	Corporal

Navy

Master chief petty officer of the Navy should follow the full name: John Paul Smith, master chief petty officer of the Navy; Chief Smith. Other ratings:

Before Full Name	Before Last Name Only
Master Chief Petty Officer	Chief
Senior Chief Petty Officer	Chief
Chief Petty Officer	Chief
Petty Officer 1st Class	Petty Officer
Petty Officer 2nd Class	Petty Officer
Petty Officer 3rd Class	Petty Officer
Seaman	Seaman
Seaman Apprentice	Seaman
Seaman Recruit	Recruit

Specialties: Navy and Coast Guard have more than 75 types of specialists who are customarily referred to by their specialties. They range from boatswain's mate to electronics warfare technician, and each specialty runs the scale of ratings from recruit to master chief. The hundreds of official acronyms are meaningless to all but a few readers, so the only abbreviation possible is omission of a few words.

Lowest rating of electronics warfare technician, for instance, is Electronics Warfare Technician Seaman Recruit Jack Tar, but for our purposes he is Electronics Warfare Recruit Jack Tar; Recruit Tar.

Taking radioman as example, the ratings are:

Before Full Name	Before Last Name	Subsequently
Master Chief Radioman	Chief	the chief
Senior Chief Radioman	Chief	the chief
Chief Radioman	Chief	the chief
Radioman 1st Class	Radioman	the radioman
Radioman 2nd Class	Radioman	the radioman
Radioman 3rd Class	Radioman	the radioman
Radioman Seaman	Seaman	the seaman
Radioman Apprentice	Apprentice	the apprentice
Radioman Recruit	Recruit	the recruit

EXAMPLE: Master Chief Radioman Bill Budd; Chief Budd; the chief

NOTE: Specialists beginning with 3rd Class actually hold the parallel ratings of petty officers, chief petty officers, etc., but they usually are styled by their specialties nevertheless.

Air Force

Chief master sergeant of the Air Force should follow the name: Seth Wright, chief master sergeant of the Air Force; Sergeant Wright. Other ratings:

Before Full Name	Before Last Name Only
Chief Master Sgt.	Sergeant
Senior Master Sgt.	Sergeant
Master Sgt.	Sergeant
Technical Sgt.	Sergeant
Staff Sgt.	Sergeant
Sgt.	Sergeant
Airman 1st Class	Airman
Airman	Airman
Airman Basic	Airman

NOTE: When referring to ranks only, without a person, lower-case: a general, generals; a sergeant, sergeants. But when referring to named officers or servicemen in the plural, it's Gens. John Muntz and George Abercrombie; Warrant Officers Fred Jones and Haller Brown.

Weights and Measures—Traditional

3.15   Most of the abbreviations below are used only in maps, charts, boxes. But *B.t.u.*, *hp*, *kw*, *kwh*, *mpg*, *mph*, *psi* and *rpm* may be used in running copy after the words have once been spelled out.

bbl.—barrel or barrels

B.t.u.—British thermal unit,—s

bu.—bushel,—s

cal.—calorie, —s

dol., dols.—dollar,—s

ft.—foot, feet

gal.—gallon, —s

hp—horsepower

hr.—hour, —s

in.—inch, —es

kw—kilowatt, —s

kwh—kilowatt-hour, —s

lb.—pound, —s

min.—minute,—s

mpg—miles per gallon

mile, miles—no abbreviations

mph—miles per hour

oz.—ounce, —s

psi—pounds per square inch

qtr., q—quarter

rpm—revolutions per minute

sec.—second, —s

ton, tons—no abbreviations

yd.—yard, —s

yr.—year, —s

Weights and Measures—Metric

3.16   (Explanations and tables in this section are taken from "Metric Style Guide for the News Media," published by the National Bureau of Standards. A few adjustments have been made to accommodate *USN&WR* methods of writing and abbreviation.)

In most cases, familiarity with the following metric units will be sufficient for everyday transactions:

	Name	Symbol	Approximate Size
length	meter	m	39½ inches
	kilometer	km	0.6 mile
	centimeter	cm	width of a paper clip
	millimeter	mm	thickness of paper clip
area	hectare	ha	2½ acres
weight	gram	g	weight of a paper clip
	kilogram	kg	2.2 pounds
	metric ton	t	long ton (2240 pounds)
volume	liter	L	one quart and 2 ounces
	milliliter	mL	⅕ teaspoon
pressure	kilopascal	kPa	atmospheric pressure is about 100 kPa

Units of time and electricity will not change.

The Celsius temperature scale should be used. Familiar points:

	°C	°F
Freezing point of water	0	32
Boiling point of water	100	212
Normal body temperature	37	98.6
Comfortable room temperature	20-25	68-77

Prefixes. Some of the metric units listed at the start of this section include prefixes such as *kilo-*, *centi-* and *milli-*. Prefixes, added to a unit name, create larger or smaller units by factors that are powers of 10. For example, add the prefix *kilo-*, which means a thousand, to the unit *gram*, to indicate 1,000 grams; thus 1,000 grams becomes 1 kilogram. The more common prefixes are shown in Table 1, on page 34.

Capitals. Names of all units start with a lower-case letter except at the beginning of a sentence. There is one exception: in *degrees Celsius* the unit *degrees* is lower case but the modifier *Celsius* is capitalized.

Symbols for units are lc except for liter and those units derived from the name of a person (*m* for *meter* but *W* for *watt*, *Pa* for *pascal*, etc.)

Symbols for prefixes that mean a million or more are capped and those for less than a million are lc (*M* for *mega*, *k* for *kilo*).

Plurals. Names of units are made plural only when the numerical value that precedes them is more than 1. For example, *0.25 liter* or *¼ liter* but *250 milliliters*.

Symbols for units are never pluralized *(250 mm)*.

Spacing. A space is left between the number and the symbol to which it refers *(7 m; 31.4 kg)*.

In names or symbols for units having prefixes, no space is left between the letters making up the symbol and those making up the name *(milligram, mg; kilometer, km)*.

Period. Do not use a period with metric-unit names and symbols except at the end of a sentence.

Conversions. Conversions should follow a rule of reason: Don't include figures that imply more accuracy than justified by the original data. For example, 36 inches would be converted to 91 centimeters, and 40.1 inches would convert to 101.9 centimeters, not 101.854. Table 2 on page 35 lists many of the more commonly used conversion factors.

For more detail. Approximate conversions for many units are given in Table 2. Some writers and editors will want more information on units in other fields. For example, the British thermal unit, calorie and therm are replaced by the metric *joule*. Further help is available in "NBS Guidelines for Use of the Metric System," LC1056, a free booklet published by the Bureau of Standards. A copy is kept on the *USN&WR* Name Checker's desk.

Table 1
COMMON PREFIXES FOR METRIC UNITS

Factor	Prefix	Symbol
1,000,000	mega	M
1,000	kilo	k
1/100	centi	c
1/1,000	milli	m
1/1,000,000	micro*	μ*

* No contraction for the prefix *micro* can be used unless the Greek letter *mu* is available to you.

Table 2
METRIC CONVERSION FACTORS (approximate)

When You Know Number of	Multiply by	To Find Number of	Symbol
LENGTH			
inches	2.54	centimeters	cm
feet	30	centimeters	cm
yards	0.9	meters	m
miles	1.6	kilometers	km
AREA			
square inches	6.5	square centimeters	squ cm
square feet	0.09	square meters	squ m
square yards	0.8	square meters	squ m
square miles	2.6	square kilometers	squ km
acres	0.4	hectares	ha
WEIGHT (Mass)			
ounces	28	grams	g
pounds	0.45	kilograms	kg
short tons (2000 pounds)	0.9	metric tons	t
VOLUME			
teaspoons	5	milliliters	mL
tablespoons	15	milliliters	mL
cubic inches	16	milliliters	mL
fluid ounces	30	milliliters	mL
cups	0.24	liters	L
pints	0.47	liters	L
quarts	0.95	liters	L
gallons	3.8	liters	L
cubic feet	0.03	cubic meters	cu m
cubic yards	0.76	cubic meters	cu m
PRESSURE			
inches of mercury	3.4	kilopascals	kPa
pounds per square inch	6.9	kilopascals	kPa
TEMPERATURE (exact)			
degrees Fahrenheit	5/9 (after subtracting 32)	degrees Celsius	°C

When to abbreviate. In most cases, metric terms should be spelled out the first time used. Thereafter, abbreviation is all right if it suits the tone of the article. Some measures, such as those of guns, are abbreviated from the start: *77-mm gun, 7.3-mm pistol.*

Miscellaneous Abbreviations

3.17 ABM—formed from "antiballistic missile," but that is an incorrect expression. Do not abbreviate in first-time use; write "anti-ballistic-missile system" or "antimissile missile."

AT&T; but: ITT

bil., for billion,—s (charts, boxes, maps)

c.o.d.

Company names:

Co. (charts, boxes, maps)

Corp. (charts, boxes, maps)

Ltd.

& Co. (*& Company* in running copy)

& Bro., & Bros.

(D-Wyo.), etc., after names of Senators and Representatives

D or Dem. (charts, boxes, maps)

f.o.b.

FDR

GI, GI's (lc *s* even in all-cap heads)

GOP

ID

IOU

IQ

ITT; but: AT&T

JFK

mdse. (charts, boxes, maps)

mfg.—manufacturing (charts, boxes, maps)

mfr., mfrs.—manufacture, —s; manufacturer, —s (charts, boxes, maps)

mil., for million, —s (charts, boxes, maps)

MIRV—multiple, independently targeted re-entry vehicle (use only with explanation)

mo.—month, —s (charts, boxes, maps)

MP—military police

M.P.—member of Parliament

mph—miles per hour

NAACP

NCO, NCO's—noncommissioned officer, officers

No., Nos. (before figures)

O.K., O.K.'d, O.K.'ing

q.—quarter (charts, boxes, maps); in table stub: Q

(R-Va.), etc., after names of Senators and Representatives

R or Rep.—Republican (charts, boxes, maps)

Rep.—Representative (in series, charts, boxes, maps—but only when it cannot be mistaken for Republican)

R.R.—Railroad (charts, boxes, maps)

Ry.—Railway (charts, boxes, maps)

SOS

TNT

V-E Day

V-J Day

vs.—versus (both letters lc in all headlines except at start of line, in which case it is Vs.)

v.—in legal citations: *Jones v. NLRB* (italicize legal citations)

NOTES

CAPITALIZATION

Government

4.0   *government* and *administration* are lower-cased except in names of agencies, companies, etc.:

the U.S. government	the federal government
the Italian government	the Goldoni administration
Government Printing Office	Government Consultants, Inc.

4.1   *nation, national, federal* are lower-cased except when part of capitalized names:

all around the nation   the Federal Energy Administration

the federal Department of Labor (*federal* not part of name)

4.2   *Union, Republic, the States* are capitalized when referring to the United States, or when part of a name; otherwise lower-cased. Lower-case *colonies.* Lower-case state except when part of a name.

the state of Nebraska	Hawaii is the 50th state
the states of the Union	on return to the States
in defense of the Republic (U.S.)	State Liquors, Inc.
the colonies revolted in 1775	

4.3   *cabinet,* referring to an advisory council of a government, is lower-cased:

the U.S. cabinet   the Goldoni cabinet

4.4   *brain trust* is lower-cased.

4.5   **Names of departments** and agencies are capitalized; generic words such as *department, board, agency* are lower-cased when used alone:

Department of State *or* State Department; the department

the Departments of State and Agriculture

the State and Agriculture departments

Agency for International Development; the agency

Federal Reserve Board; the board

Internal Revenue Service; the Revenue Service; the service

Office of Management and Budget; the Budget Office; the office

4.6 **Subdivisions** of government agencies and departments are lower-cased:

> the division of labor relations of ERA
>
> the antitrust division of the Justice Department

4.7 **National legislative terms** are treated as follows:

> Congress; congressional
>
> the U.S. Senate; senatorial
>
> the House of Representatives; the House
>
> the houses of Congress; either house of Congress

4.8 NOTE: Regardless of widespread use, it is inaccurate to refer to the House of Representatives as the lower house. Maybe the custom developed with regard to the British Parliament, when lords were all-important and commoners were lowly, but it is no longer appropriate and should be avoided. The House is certainly no lower than the Senate. It is even further from the mark to call the German Bundestag the lower house, or to call the Bundesrat, which is roughly equivalent to the Senate, the upper house. Almost all the power is in the Bundestag.

4.9 **Committees and subcommittees** of Congress are capitalized, but *committee* and *subcommittee* are lower-cased in subsequent reference. Do not capitalize *committee* or *subcommittee* if the name of the group has not been used.

> Committee on Banking and Currency; the committee
>
> Joint Committee on Defense Production; the committee
>
> Internal Security Subcommittee; the subcommittee
>
> the Senate committee that deals with postal affairs

4.10 **Foreign national and United Nations** legislative bodies are treated in the same way as American.

> United Nations Security Council; the Council (equivalent to U.S. Senate)
>
> British Parliament; Parliament
>
> House of Commons; the Commons
>
> the Japanese Diet; the Diet
>
> French National Assembly; the Assembly

Lower-case *the parliament* referring to a foreign assembly when that is not its name.

4.11   **States, counties, cities** and their governmental bodies follow generally the same pattern as federal.

> the state of Georgia; the state   New York City; the city
>
> Tazewell County; the county   Montgomery and Fairfax counties
>
> the Virginia State Corporation Commission; the commission
>
> the Maryland Department of Health and Mental Hygiene; the department
>
> the Montgomery County Landlord-Tenant Affairs Office; the office
>
> the Fairfax County Board of Supervisors; the board
>
> the New York City Council; the council

4.12   **State legislatures** and their divisions are capitalized. The term generally used is *Legislature,* even if the state calls its legislative body the General Assembly, the General Court or something else. These other names may be used if the writer wishes to do so for some special reason such as local color, but with care to prevent the New Hampshire General Court from being mistaken for a court, or the Connecticut General Assembly from being confused with the kind of assembly that usually is just one house of a legislature.

    The separate houses of any legislature—Senate, Assembly, House of Representatives, House of Delegates—are capitalized.

> the New York Legislature; the New York State Legislature; the Legislature
>
> the New Hampshire Legislature; the New Hampshire General Court—the state's legislature—debated . . .
>
> In the New Hampshire Legislature, the House of Representatives passed . . . The House then . . .
>
> the New Hampshire House of Representatives
>
> the State Legislature; a state legislature
>
> the legislatures of Maine and Vermont

    Committees of state legislatures should be treated the same way as committees of Congress.

4.13   **Names of courts** are capitalized; *court* is lower-cased in subsequent mention except when reference is to the Supreme

Court of the United States:

> the United States Supreme Court; the High Court; the Court

> the United States Court of Appeals for the First Circuit covers the districts of Vermont, northern New York, etc.; the court

> the Arkansas Supreme Court; the court

> the Municipal Court of Chicago; the court

> the Circuit Court of Montgomery County; the court

When used merely in description and not as a name, *court* is lower-cased:

> I have to go down to traffic court although I didn't do anything.

> Most 17-year-olds when arrested are sent to juvenile court.

When *Court* is used to mean the judge on the bench, it is capitalized:

> The Court reprimanded the prosecutor for her language.

4.14   *Social Security* is capitalized when referring to the U.S. system; lower-cased in reference to systems abroad or in a philosophical sense:

> your Social Security check   in favor of social security

> And social security is universal in Sweden.

4.15   *Civil Service* is capitalized in reference to the Civil Service Commission, lower-cased when applied to the system of civil service and government workers within that system:

> Civil Service employes (work for the commission)

> civil-service employes (work for the government under civil-service regulations)

Government Actions and Documents

4.16   *Act* is capitalized when part of a name, lower-cased on subsequent mention or standing alone:

> Immigration and Nationality Act; the act

> an act of Congress; acts of Congress

4.17   **Names of bills and laws** are lower-cased except for popular appellations that are unclear in themselves; the words *bill* and *law* are generally lower-cased even in capitalized names:

this year's civil-rights bill	the tax-reform bill
Kennedy-Brooke bill	the Sunset bill
the Sunshine in Government bill	
the immigration and nationality law	

BUT note these exceptions:

Corn Laws (historical)	GI Bill	Bill of Rights

4.18 *Code* is capitalized when used with an official title, lower-cased when used in a general sense.

civil code	Federal Criminal Code
Internal Revenue Code; the code	

4.19 **Administrative documents** are capitalized when they are titles, lower-cased when not.

The President carried out the policy by executive order.

The President today issued Executive Order 107.

The President issued an executive order.

today's papal bull

a white paper from the State Department

4.20 *Constitution* is capitalized when referring to the Constitution of the United States or a state or a foreign government:

the U.S. Constitution; the Constitution

the French Constitution; the Constitution

the Arkansas Constitution; the Constitution

United Nations

4.21 (The abbreviation is styled: U.N.)

Security Council; the Council (equivalent to a nation's Senate)

General Assembly; the Assembly (equivalent to a nation's House)

Secretary-General; the Secretary-General

the secretariat (roughly equivalent to a cabinet)

United Nations Charter; the Charter (equivalent to U.S. Constitution)

Organizations and agencies under the U.N. are capitalized, but on subsequent mention the generic words are lower-cased. Examples:

International Court of Justice; the court

Trusteeship Council; the council

International Monetary Fund; IMF; the fund

Political Parties

4.22   *Party* is capitalized when part of a title, lower-cased when alone. Do not capitalize in plural:

Communist Party; the party

an independent party

Republican Party; the party

Republican and Democratic parties

4.23   **Nouns and adjectives** referring to membership in political parties are capitalized:

Communist	Conservative	Republican
Socialist	Liberal	Monarchist
Know-Nothing (in 1850s)		Nazism, Nazi

4.24   **Political movements and beliefs** not tied to specific parties, as well as the people holding such beliefs and the adjectives applicable to the movements and people, are lower-cased except when derived from proper names:

communism, communist (in a philosophical sense)

Marxism, Marxist

democracy; a democracy

conservative thinking

a socialist (in thought); socialist tendencies

monarchist rumblings (BUT: the Monarchist Party)

4.25   **Conventions and officials** of political parties are lower-cased.

Republican national convention

Henry Blucher, Democratic national chairman

BUT: Republican National Committee (name of an organization; see 4.50)

Democratic National Chairman Blucher (title before name)

International Blocs, Agreements, Policies

4.26   *Allies* is capitalized only in a name or in reference to major groups that have acquired the appellation *the Allies:* the nations that opposed Germany in World Wars I and II, the present North Atlantic Treaty Organization, and any bloc of world powers that may achieve the title by general usage. The word is lower-cased when applied to partners of the U.S. in these or other groups, or to allies of any nation. To be capitalized, the word has to designate the bloc as a whole.

> the NATO Allies; the Allies; allies of the U.S. in NATO
>
> The Allies defeated the Central Powers in 1918.
>
> U.S. allies in Europe, Asia

Allied, adj., is capitalized only in reference to a group characterized as *the Allies:*

> the Allied debacle at the Somme

4.27   *Agreement, Alliance, Pact, Treaty* are capitalized as part of official names, lower-cased as part of descriptive phrases or standing alone:

> General Agreement on Tariffs and Trade; GATT; the agreement
>
> the U.S.-Canadian trade agreement
>
> Alliance for Progress; the alliance; alliance nations
>
> Atlantic Alliance (NATO); the alliance; the Allies
>
> Warsaw Pact; the pact; pact nations
>
> Treaty of Versailles; Versailles Treaty; the treaty
>
> Western Alliance (NATO)

4.28   *Doctrine* is capitalized in the recognized name of an official pronouncement, lower-cased when standing alone:

> Monroe Doctrine; the doctrine
>
> preaching an isolationist doctrine

4.29   *policy* is generally lower-cased in names of governmental lines of action, but the surrounding words are capped if the names are well established:

> the Open Door policy; an open-door policy toward Canada
>
> America's Good Neighbor policy; a good-neighbor policy among Caribbean nations
>
> Russia's New Economic Policy (official name of a regulation)
>
> Jimmy Carter's economic policy

Military

4.30   *Army, Navy, Air Force, Marine Corps* are capitalized when referring to the organization of a particular country, and when standing alone if referring to the specific organization mentioned previously:

U.S. Army, the Army	U.S. Coast Guard
U.S. Air Force	Japanese Navy; the Navy
U.S. Navy	Soviet Army; an army
U.S. Marine Corps; the Marine Corps; the Corps	

4.31   *Division, Regiment, Branch, Company, Battalion,* etc., are capitalized when used with official number or designation. Lower-case when used alone in subsequent mention. Organizations and branches of the armed forces are capitalized.

National Guard; the Guard	Naval Reserves; the Reserves
45th Division; the division	the Infantry
First Corps; the corps	Army Field Forces
Seventh Army; the army	Second Airmobile Division
Airborne Infantry	Transportation Corps
Seabees	Allied Forces Southern Europe

U.S. Army Reserves; the Reserves

U.S. Army Corps of Engineers; the corps

the Regular Army or the all-volunteer Army (they are the same, designating the permanent or standing army of the United States)

4.32   *Fleet* is capitalized when part of a name, but not in a general sense:

U.S. Fleet; the Fleet	Sixth Fleet; the fleet
a fleet in the Atlantic	

4.33   *naval* and, as adjective, *navy* are lower-cased except in a proper name:

naval officer	a navy yard
officer of the Navy	Norfolk Naval Shipyard

4.34   *U.S. merchant marine, the merchant marine* are lower-cased. But:

U.S. Merchant Marine Academy

4.35   *regular* and *volunteer* are lower-cased in a general sense:

a regular   a volunteer

4.36   **Members of individual services** are lower-cased. Exceptions: *Seabee, Green Beret,* other made-up words. (NOTE: *coast guardman,* without an *s,* is the correct official spelling.) Do not capitalize the following:

infantryman	sailor	soldier
infantry officer	artilleryman	marine

BUT: the Marines as an organization, when comparable to the Army, the Navy; Marine battalions

4.37   *military attaché, naval attaché,* etc., are lower-cased except when used before a name as a title.

4.38   *War* is capitalized in accepted names of past and current wars:

the Vietnam War, the war   the Civil War (U.S. history)

the Spanish Civil War   Korean War

the civil war in Lebanon *or* Lebanese civil war (Lebanese Civil War if it becomes historically so known)

World War I   World Wars I and II

4.39   *occupation,* meaning seizure and control by a foreign power, is lower-cased all the way:

Germany under the occupation   the occupation government

He appealed to occupation headquarters.

Titles

4.40   **All titles before names** are capitalized:

Secretary Jesse Filbert of the Ace Duce Company

Secretary of State Ralph Roney

Police Chief Charles Inscoe

4.41   **Occupational descriptions** are lower-cased:

news reporter Stanley Staunch

social worker William Branch

4.42   **Titles of officials of private firms, associations,** foundations, political organizations, etc., are not capitalized after names or on subsequent mention without names:

> Jack Filbert, chairman of the Democratic National Committee
>
> Jesse Filbert, secretary of the company, spoke. The secretary said . . .

4.43 **Government officials' titles** generally are not capitalized below cabinet rank when after names or without names, but there are exceptions. In all cases, the last name may be used without a title. Secretary of the Navy (Army, Air Force) capped when standing alone.

> the President of the United States; the President; President Wilson; choosing a President; Presidents; the Chief Executive; the Commander in Chief (but lower-case when referring to anyone except the President); also Presidency, presidential
>
> the Vice President of the U.S.; the Vice President; Vice President Rockefeller; choosing a Vice President; Vice Presidency, vice-presidential
>
> the Secretary of State; a secretary of state; Secretary of State John Mingo; the Secretary; Secretaries of State Jones and Thompson; the Secretary of the Navy; Navy Secretary
>
> Deputy Secretary of State Paul Harding; the deputy secretary; Harding
>
> Atty. Gen. A. C. Dermott; the Attorney General
>
> Chairman Fred Baynes of the Federal Reserve Board; Fred Baynes, chairman of the Federal Reserve Board; the chairman
>
> BUT NOTE: Hua Kuo-feng, Chairman of the People's Republic of China (as head of state)
>
> Budget Director Maxim Gold; Maxim Gold, director, Office of Management and Budget; the director
>
> Joseph LeSabre, director of central intelligence
>
> Chief Justice John P. Marshall; John P. Marshall, Chief Justice of the United States; the Chief Justice
>
> Associate Justice Mary Burke; Mary Burke, Associate Justice of the U.S. Supreme Court; Justice Burke; the Justice
>
> Chief Judge Harper; Cestus Harper, chief judge of the U.S. Court of Appeals for the District of Columbia; the chief judge
>
> Judge Ellen Purcell of the Palm Rest Municipal Court; the judge

Senator Genevieve Busby (D-Ala.); Genevieve Busby, the senior senator from Alabama; the senator; a senator

Representative John Doe (R-N.Y.); the representative; a representative

Jeremy Flaum of Iowa, majority leader of the Senate

president pro tem of the Senate

Speaker of the House; the Speaker (to avoid confusion over the word *speaker*)

Chairman Flaum of the Senate Foreign Relations Committee; the chairman

Governor April Forman of Idaho; Governor Forman; Forman; the governor; a governor

Lt. Gov. John Bird; the lieutenant governor

State Atty. Gen. George Benchman; the attorney general

Mayor Jack Rackstraw of Virginia City; the mayor; a mayor

Gen. Simon Delibre; the general; a general

Gen. Henry L. Clinchman, chairman of the Joint Chiefs of Staff

Gen. Bernard Blosser, Army chief of staff

Ambassador Jarrel Jester; Jarrel Jester, ambassador to the Always Isles; the ambassador; Ambassador to the U.N.

Press Secretary Harper McDaniel; the President's press secretary

4.44 **Foreign and international officials,** military commanders are styled basically the same as American:

French President Pierre Hautbrion; President Hautbrion; Hautbrion; the President

French Premier Mitzi Chambertain; Premier Chambertain; Chambertain; the Premier

British Prime Minister Egbert Foxhall; Prime Minister Foxhall; Foxhall; the Prime Minister

King Ferdinand of Spain; King Ferdinand; Ferdinand; the King

Queen Isabella of Spain; Queen Isabella; Isabella; the Queen

Prince Paul of Monaco; Prince Paul; Paul; the Prince (head of state)

Princess Margaret of Monaco; Princess Margaret; Margaret; the Princess

Prince Alfred of Britain; Alfred; the prince (not head of state)

Alfred, Prince of Wales (honorary title); the prince

Hua Kuo-feng, Chairman of the People's Republic of China; the Chairman (head of state)

French Finance Minister Arnaud de Roos; Finance Minister de Roos; de Roos; the Finance Minister

finance ministers of 12 countries

Hugo Ruff, Secretary-General of the United Nations; Secretary-General Ruff; the Secretary-General

Pope Aloysius XIII; the Pope; a pope; papal

Cardinal John Baumann; the cardinal

Archbishop Perry Green; Archbishop Green; the archbishop

the Dalai Lama
(Of religious dignitaries, only the Pope and the Dalai Lama have titles that are capitalized when standing alone.)

Gen. Rufus Fox, Supreme Allied Commander Europe (official title), BUT if desired: Gen. Rufus Fox, supreme Allied commander for Europe, or NATO commander for Europe

Adm. Aloysius Green, commander in chief, Allied Forces Southern Europe (using words as official name of unit), BUT: Adm. Aloysius Green, commander in chief of Allied forces in southern Europe (descriptive)

His Majesty, Your Majesty, Your Grace, Your Honor, Your Excellency; my lord (l.c.): I fear you are in error, my lord.

4.45 **Nobility** is styled in the following pattern:

Wilhelm, Duke of Brunswick; Duke Wilhelm; Wilhelm; the duke

Anthony Eden, Earl of Avon; Eden; the earl

Count Georg von Hertling; Hertling; the count

Baron John Hugo Russell of Ampthill; Russell; the baron

Sir Walter Scott, Bart.; Scott; Sir Walter; the baronet

Religion

4.46 **Names of God,** the Supreme Being, are capitalized. Examples: Allah, God, Jehovah.

Names of lesser gods also are capitalized: Apollo, Adonis, Juno, Aphrodite, etc.

Pronouns for God: *He, His, Him* are capitalized, but not *who, whose, whom.*

Appellations meaning God, though not official names, are capitalized. Examples:

> the Almighty, the Father, the King of Kings, the Lamb of God, the Lord, the Prince of Peace, the Son of God

4.47 **Personages** in religious lore or history are capitalized. Examples:

> the Baptist, the Blessed Virgin, Buddha, Messiah, Mother of God, our Lady, the Prophet (meaning Muhammad), Queen of Heaven, the Virgin, the Virgin Mary.

4.48 **Religious denominations** are capitalized. The word *church* is lower-cased in subsequent mention:

> the Roman Catholic Church; the church
>
> the Episcopal Church; the church

4.49 **Individual churches** are capitalized:

> Grace and Holy Trinity Episcopal Church; the church
>
> an Episcopal church; the Episcopal church next door
>
> Beth El Temple; the temple

(For answers to other questions of religious style, see "Church and Clergy," 10.0 to 10.16.)

Committees

(For congressional committees, see 4.9.)

4.50 *Committee* in the name of an organization or official group is capitalized:

> Democratic National Committee; the committee
>
> Republican National Committee; the committee
>
> President's Committee on Employment of the Handicapped; the committee
>
> Committee for Economic Development; the committee

4.51   **Committees of organizations** are lower-cased:

> finance committee of the Democratic National Committee
>
> executive committee of the American Antiquarian Society

Organizations and Functions

4.52   *Company, Corporation, Foundation, Association, Society* are capitalized when part of a name but lower-cased when standing alone.

> Ford Motor Company; the company
>
> Ford Foundation; the foundation
>
> National Association of Manufacturers; the association
>
> E. I. du Pont de Nemours & Company; the Du Pont Company; Du Pont; the company

4.53   *Council* and similar words are capitalized in the name of an organization or agency but lower-cased when describing the function of a group. Lower-case when standing alone.

> the Business Council; the council
>
> the St. Louis Chamber of Commerce; the chamber
>
> the Council on Foreign Relations; the council
>
> the executive council of the AFL-CIO
>
> BUT NOTE: United Nations Security Council; the Council (equivalent of a national Senate)

4.54   *Department, Division:* Capitalize as part of the name of a primary agency of a government; capitalize as part of the name of a company; lower-case if part of the name of a subdivision of a company or agency:

> Department of Justice; antitrust division of the Justice Department
>
> Rademacher's Department Store; the clothing department
>
> Virginia Division of Motor Vehicles; the division
>
> Chevrolet division of General Motors
>
> industrial-union department of AFL-CIO

Lower-case departments of schools and colleges when the words are merely descriptive.

> the Yale history department

4.55 **In names of magazines,** do not capitalize (or italicize) *magazine* unless it is part of the name.
(More on names of publications in 5.39, 5.40, 5.55-5.57.)

4.56 *Union* is capitalized when used as part of the name or of an accepted paraphrase, but lower-cased when standing alone or in a merely descriptive phrase:

> United Automobile, Aerospace and Agricultural Implement Workers of America (we don't ordinarily use this); United Auto Workers Union; United Auto Workers; Auto Workers Union; the auto union; the union

4.57 *Conference* or an equivalent word is capitalized when part of a full official name. But do not capitalize when the accompanying word or words are only a place name or a place name and a date. Do not capitalize when accompanied by descriptive words that do not make up an official title; sometimes mere descriptions are inadvertently raised to official status. There will be borderline cases requiring judgment. Often the context will determine. Explanatory phrases may be called for.

> the Geneva conference of 1954; in 1954, the Geneva conference on Far Eastern affairs . . .
>
> the International Conference on Extermination of Rats; the world conference on rodents; the conference
>
> Congress of Vienna; the congress
>
> the Hamburg symposium on protection of seacoasts against pollution
>
> the Itinerant Symposium on the Granites of Northeast; the symposium

Note that *summit* and *summit conference* have taken on generic status through frequent use and need not be capitalized. Be sparing of *summit* alone to mean a summit conference, as "they held a summit in Madagascar"; it is illogical and has lost its novelty.

> the economic summit conference at Rambouillet in 1975; the Rambouillet summit conference
>
> a conference at the summit; a meeting at the summit

Education

4.58 *College, University, School, Academy, Institute,* etc. are capitalized when part of a name. Do not capitalize when standing alone.

> Harvard University; the university
>
> St. John's College; the college
>
> Pratt Institute; the institute
>
> McLean High School   the high school at McLean

4.59 **Divisions of a college, university,** etc. are capitalized when part of a name, lower-cased when expressing a function; departments ordinarily are lower-cased on the assumption that the words are functional:

> Harvard Law School; Harvard's law school; the law school at Harvard
>
> the Harvard history department

4.60 **Academic degrees** and related honors are capitalized when abbreviated or when applied to specific persons, lower-cased when used generally or separated from persons:

> the title of LL.D.   a doctor-of-laws degree
>
> J. B. Smith, Doctor of Laws   J. B. Smith, LL.D.
>
> Derek Fothergill, fellow of the Royal Academy; elected a fellow of the Royal Academy

4.61 *Scholarship, Fellowship* are capitalized when the name of the award is used; *scholar, fellow* are lower-cased:

> a Rhodes Scholarship; a Rhodes scholar
>
> a Niemann Fellowship; a Niemann fellow
>
> a fellow at Harvard

4.62 **School subjects:** Except in reference to specific courses, capitalize only those words that are names of languages or other proper names:

> mathematics   calculus   Latin   Greek
>
> English history   Literature II

4.63 **Titles of professors and school officials** are capitalized before names, but lower-cased after names and when appearing alone:

> Jervis P. Boulanger, president of Bainbridge University
>
> Prof. John Altergarten; Professor Altergarten; John Altergarten, professor of English; the professor
>
> BUT: John Altergarten, Edgar Allen Poe Professor of English

Geographic Terms

4.64   *east, west, north, south, northeast, southwest,* etc. are lower-cased when indicating mere direction or location:

> The suspect ran east.

> A vast region lies to the west of the Mississippi.

East, West, North, South, Southwest, etc. are capitalized when used alone to designate portions of the world, the continents, nations and states:

> The East is a mystery to the rest of the world.

> Africa's West harbors a profusion of animals.

> The Republicans lost seven states in the South.

Capitalize also combinations such as Middle East, Mideast, Far West.

When *East, West,* etc. are used as modifiers in recognized official names or as parts of familiar appellations for geographical areas, they are capitalized.

West Germany	Southwest Virginia	Southwest Pacific
North Africa	East Tennessee	West Bank (of the Jordan)

Confine this usage to recognized appellations. Do not, for instance, make up a term like "East Virginia"; use instead "eastern Virginia."

Adjectives derived from regional terms are capitalized when referring to a region's people or characteristics:

> Southern customs   Midwestern states   the Eastern enigma

When referring to officially named regions, or areas with widely accepted traditional appellations, or when applied to groups with established names, *Eastern, Western,* etc. are capitalized.

> Eastern Hemisphere   Western Allies   Western World
>
> Eastern Shore of Maryland or Virginia   Southern Illinois
>
> Southern California   Northern California
>
> Eastern or Western Europe (political rather than geographic)

But when referring to regions not clearly defined or not bearing established appellations, do not capitalize.

> northeastern Nebraska   western Africa   eastern Iran

4.65   *Central, Upper, Lower, Middle* are capitalized when part of a proper name or generally accepted appellation, but lower-cased when merely descriptive.

> Upper Michigan   Upper Peninsula of Michigan
>
> central North America   Central America
>
> Lower California (for Baja California)

4.66   **Antarctica, Arctic Circle,** the Arctic, the Antarctic, Arctic Ocean, Arctic Current, arctic temperatures, arctic conditions (follow these styles).

4.67   *State, Canton, Province* are capitalized only when part of a name:

> the Empire State
>
> state of California, the state; the states of the United States
>
> canton of Berne, the canton; cantons of Switzerland
>
> province of Quebec, the province; provinces of Canada
>
> Washington State, New York State

4.68   **Political divisions** such as congressional districts and wards and precincts are lower-cased:

> the third congressional district   the fourth ward
>
> Chesterbrook precinct

4.69   **Areas or imaginary locations having special names** are capitalized.

> the Delta   Badlands   Southern Highlands
>
> Death Valley   Big Bend   Everglades
>
> Panhandle   Black Hills   Rockies, Smokies
>
> Black Forest   Upstate New York Twin Cities
>
> Border states   Lower 48   The Downs
>
> the Promised Land   Lake District (England)

BUT combinations with *belt* are lc: corn belt, black belt, farm belt. In Bible belt, if it must be used in a text, quote, etc., cap *Bible* only.

4.70   *Island, Peninsula, Mountain, Bay, Gulf, River, Dam* and similar words are capitalized when part of a name. Lower-case when standing alone, even in reference to a place just named.

> the Iberian Peninsula (Peninsula part of name)
>
> the Italian peninsula (not part of name)

Marianas Islands; the islands   Grand Coulee Dam; the dam

Mississippi River; the river   the Mississippi and Ohio rivers

Mobjack Bay; the bay

Exceptions are made for some geographical entities with a tradition of solo appearance, where identity is clear:

In Texas, much industry is concentrated along the Gulf.

Leaving England, he crossed the Channel to Cherbourg.

4.71   *coast* is lower-cased when referring to the shoreline, capitalized when referring to a region of the U.S. along the coast:

The Pacific coast is dotted with rocky islands.

Pacific Coast industries   Pacific Coast states

4.72   *World:* the world, Western World, the Third World, New World, Old World (follow these styles).

Heavenly Bodies

4.73   *sun* and *moon* are lower-cased except in titles, at the beginning of sentences, and when used—without *the*—in connection with other bodies in space.

4.74   *earth* is lower-cased except in titles, when personified, or when in conjunction with other heavenly bodies:

the earth and the moon have a special relationship

Earth and Moon endlessly face each other

. . . and Earth is a lonely planet

the trip from Earth to Jupiter

the trip from the earth to Jupiter

from the moon to the earth

down to earth

4.75   **Named entities in space**—planets, stars, constellations, etc.—are capitalized; generic portions of names are generally lower-cased:

the constellation Cassiopeia   Arcturus

Satellite VII of Jupiter   Mars's moon Phobos

Phobos, one of Mars's moons

Halley's comet   the Crab nebula   the Magellanic clouds

Headlines

4.76   In upper-and-lower-case headlines and captions, all words are capitalized except the prepositions *at, by, for, in, of, on* and *to;* the conjunctions *and, but, as* and *or;* and the articles *a, an* and *the.* These words are capitalized, however, when they start any line of a head.

Also, when *at, by, for, in, of, on* or *to* comes after a verb but is not followed by an object, it is capitalized:

> What Goes On?   Filbert Is Passed By for Nomination
>
> Slur Was Uncalled For, President Says
>
> What Was the Senator Thinking Of?

In column headings of tabular matter, unlike headlines, these words are not capitalized at the start of lines unless they would be capitalized within a line. This rule is followed because it is sometimes necessary, mechanically, to rearrange the lines on short notice.

In the table of contents, *at, by, the,* etc. are capitalized after a colon if they start a full sentence, lower-cased if they start matter less than a full sentence. Contents, unlike headlines, capitalizes these words at the beginning of a second line only if they would be capitalized within a single line.

> Congress vs. President:
> The Thrill Is Gone
>
> Congress vs. President:
> the Never-Ending Fight

In hyphened combinations of words, such as *size-up,* both words are capitalized in a head. In words with hyphened prefixes, such as pre-empt, do not capitalize the second part.

In all-cap headlines and captions, *Mc* has a lower-case *c* and *Mac* has lower-case *ac;* expressions such as GI's, IQ's, TV's have a lower case *s.*

Lower-case *vs.* in upper-and-lower-case and all-cap headlines, except at start of a line. Spell *Vs.* at the start of a line.

Miscellaneous

4.77   **Addresses:** Capitalize *Alley, Avenue, Circle, Place, Road, Street, Square* and similar words when used in addresses. Do not abbreviate. Capitalize the plural form if it designates a specific location, but not if used in a general sense. Do not capitalize such words when standing alone:

Fifth Avenue   24th and N Streets, N.W.

between E and F streets

the streets of New York   an avenue in Amsterdam

4.78   **After colon:** Capitalize the first word.

He put it this way: The answer is final.

What they sought was: A final answer.

His objective was obvious: To win the war.

Why did the chicken cross the road? Answer: To get to the other side.

He bought: Five horses, 15 cows.

4.79   **Book titles:** Follow the capitalization used by the book itself:

The House of Seven Gables   *The Naked Ape*

4.80   **Buildings, monuments,** public places: These are generally capitalized—

the Capitol	Statler-Hilton Hotel
Lafayette Park	Lafayette and Potomac parks
the Mall (Washington)	Eisenhower Theater at the Kennedy Center
Jefferson Memorial	Key Bridge
Union Station	Brandenburg Gate
the Statue of Liberty	the statue of Kennedy
the Blue Room	Russian Embassy; the embassy

4.81   **Before numerals and letters,** capitalize terms such as *Appendix, Chapter, Class, Exhibit, Figure, Form, Group, Highway, Model, No., Plate, Room, Schedule, Table.* Do not capitalize *page.*

Examples below do not indicate preference for Roman or Arabic numerals.

Article I	Figure IV	Room 320
Chapter II	page XIII	Section 2
Table 2	Highway 9	Schedule D
Plate 9	Model 3C	Appendix A
Form 1040		

4.82   **Adaptations** of proper nouns and adjectives to specialized uses sometimes drop initial capitals, sometimes retain them:

pasteurize	Roman numerals	roman type

Many of the most common such terms are in the Word List. Follow the dictionary for all others.

4.83   **Cultural designations**—philosophical, literary, musical, etc.—are usually lower-cased unless derived from proper names or in some other special situation that calls for capitalization. But in some cases, derivation from a proper noun does not mean capitalize. Go by the dictionary. A sampling:

baroque	impressionism	Romanesque
Corinthian	pointillism	scholasticism
Darwinian	pop concert	sophist
existentialism	realism	surrealism

Sturm und Drang (because of German capitalization)

4.84   **Holidays, special days, special weeks, etc.** are capitalized:

Christmas	Easter Sunday	New Year's Eve
Christmas Eve	Good Friday	Holy Week
Passover	Lent	Yom Kippur
Armistice Day	Mother's Day	Bastille Day
Veterans Day	Election Day	Inauguration Day
	National Safety Week	

4.85   **Historic events** are capitalized in many cases:

Boston Tea Party	Battle of Bull Run

4.86   **Historic periods**—commonly used combinations of Age, Era, etc.—are capitalized in combination, but not *century:*

Elizabethan Age	Space Age	Jazz Era
Mauve Decade	Renaissance	Age of Reason
Roaring Twenties	Restoration	Christian Era
	20th century	

4.87   **Weather phenomena** are capitalized when personified:

Hurricane Hazel	Tropical Storm Agnes

4.88   **Seasons** are not capitalized unless personified:

spring	autumn (or fall)	winter solstice

when Autumn came on in her bright garments

4.89   **Prizes, medals and awards** with set names are generally capitalized; awards representing levels of victory in track meets, fairs, and so on are lower-cased:

the Good Conduct Medal	Legion of Merit
Pulitzer Prize for fiction	Silver Star
Nobel Prize in literature	Purple Heart
Nobel Peace Prize	Medal of Freedom

Medal of Honor (no longer Congressional)

silver medal in the 100-meter dash

blue ribbon for best yearling bull

(For scholarship, fellowship, see 4.61.)

4.90   **Time:** Follow these styles—

standard time	daylight saving time
Greenwich mean time	eastern standard time
central standard time	mountain standard time
eastern daylight time	Pacific daylight time
EST, EDT, etc.	

4.91   **Weights and measures,** including metric terms, present questions in capitalization. These are dealt with in 3.15 and 3.16.

4.92   **Plurals:** When a common noun follows two or more names with which it is combined, the noun is lower-cased.

the Keystone and Prudential buildings

the Rappahannock and Potomac rivers

Yale and Harvard universities

the State and Interior departments

BUT: When the noun precedes the capitalized names, it is capitalized:

the Departments of State and Interior

the Universities of Michigan and California

Mounts Monadnock and McKinley

4.93   *Yes* and *no,* if quoted, should be capitalized:

The answer is yes.

The answer is "Yes."

(Same for *no.*)

NOTES

PUNCTUATION

5.0   The main purpose of punctuation is to separate the parts of sentences, paragraphs and whole articles in such a way that the parts and their relationship will be quickly recognizable to the reader. Punctuation is to make things clear. If it makes things confused, change it or get rid of it. Punctuation should be used where needed, but the fastest-reading news copy is constructed to need only a minimum.

Comma

5.1   Commas have standard uses in identifying and separating the parts of sentences, clauses and phrases. In some such cases the comma can be omitted without harm. It sometimes is inserted where not needed structurally but where a pause is desired for clarity—which often means the sentence is awkward and should be rewritten.

5.2   **Coordinate clauses** in a compound sentence usually are separated by a comma:

> The Premier resigned, and the King fled.

In a short sentence of that type, where clarity is not diminished the comma could be left out:

> The Premier resigned and the King fled.

But in a long compound sentence, or a short one where confusion might arise, the comma may be essential:

> WRONG: Jones murdered Smith and Anderson robbed a bank.

(Until the reader readjusts at the word *robbed*, the impression is that Jones murdered Smith and Anderson. A comma is needed.)
And a bad example from a great newspaper:

> WRONG: The wreckage from the plane was scattered all over the yard and the first floor of the house also was damaged.

(Until the end of the sentence, the reader has to think that the wreckage was scattered over the first floor as well as the yard. A comma is needed.)

5.3 **Subordinate clauses**, likewise, usually are set off by commas when they appear before the main clause. These commas too may sometimes be omitted:

> Although commas are useful, they may sometimes be omitted.

> Although commas are useful they may sometimes be omitted.

5.4 **Descriptive clauses** are surrounded by commas:

> Senator Blank, who drives a Jaguar, opposes a duty on autos.

Restrictive clauses are NOT set off by commas:

> The man who said that was undermining foreign policy.

5.5 **Introductory words and phrases** usually are set off by commas:

> Finally, police used water cannon to drive off the students.

Often such a comma can be omitted without damage.

5.6 **Parenthetical words, phrases or clauses** usually are set off by commas:

> Subordinate clauses, likewise, are set off.

> or: Subordinate clauses likewise are set off.

> A vote of no confidence, he said, would mean ruin.

After *and* or *but* or *that* at the beginning of a sentence or clause, the comma before the parenthetical matter may be omitted if the sentence remains clear:

> And if he flew to Jaffa, he would be arrested there.

5.7 **Items in a series** are divided by commas. Normally, no comma appears before the final *and:*

> On his farm he grew soybeans, peanuts and corn.

To avoid ambiguity, however, a comma before the final *and* may be needed:

> Three big industries are copper, iron and steel, and cattle.

5.8   **Where words are omitted,** commas may be substituted:

> Filbert won 42 percent of the vote; Brown, 23 percent.

Note, however, that if the parts are short and the connection clear, the commas showing omissions are not mandatory:

> Filbert won 42 percent of the vote, Brown 23 percent.

5.9   **A person's residence or workplace** is not ordinarily set off by commas:

> Rex Filbert of the Budd Company said . . .
>
> Rex Filbert of Galax, Va., said . . .
>
> Governor Rex Filbert of Alabama
>
> Senator Rex Filbert (R-Ala.) spoke . . .
>
> Senator Filbert of Alabama

5.10   **Before ZIP codes,** no comma is used:

> Washington, D.C. 20037

5.11   **A forced pause** engineered by a comma is a bad expedient. An example from a great newspaper:

> One of the things that troubles many Carter observers, that makes even those who want to believe in him, edgy, is all this love, human kindness, compassion, honesty, sincerity stuff.

Aside from a boring mistake in number, this sentence is sick enough to call for a compassionate comma—which the writer supplied without curing the sickness.

5.12   *Plus* does not require a preceding comma unless the cadence and structure of the sentence call for it:

> Intelligence plus luck pulled him through.
>
> Intelligence, plus a strong element of luck, won out.

5.13   **Other uses** of the comma:

> On Aug. 7, 1910, he was born.
>
> In April, 1977, he shot a bear.
>
> In fourth quarter, 1977, he made a profit.
>
> Chicago, Ill.
>
> 4,760,200
>
> 2300 N Street, N.W., Washington, D.C. 20037

5.14   **Overuse of commas** can be destructive. Since the function of the comma is to break up a sentence into parts whose relationships are clear, insertion of additional commas may lose or confuse the relationships. Two examples from actual copy:

> WRONG: When the best farmland is converted to other purposes, agriculture is forced to less-productive acreage, and the cost of food production rises.

Everything after the first comma is part of what happens when the best land is converted. The second comma should be omitted.

> WRONG: To ease the strain on pinched borrowers, credit companies, banks and finance houses have stretched out payment schedules.

The first comma sets aside the purpose of the action told in the second part of the sentence. But the commas in the series are piled on, making it seem that pinched borrowers, credit companies, banks, etc. are all parts of the same series. Since the structure of the sentence creates this problem, rewriting is necessary:

> To ease the strain on pinched borrowers, payment schedules have been stretched out by . . .

Semicolon

5.15   The semicolon is a useful article of punctuation that fell into disrepute, then made a comeback. It serves in most places where a somewhat more authoritative stop than a comma is needed.

5.16   **In a compound sentence,** a semicolon achieves a pleasing balance:

> Filbert plugged for bigger spending; Brown urged budget cuts.

Semicolons in this type of sentence can add interest and variety to copy. Overuse, however, could produce a formal style that reads like an essay. Care should be observed also to avoid merely stringing ideas together with semicolons when their relationship really needs more explanation.

5.17   **Division between phrases** that already have commas should be made with semicolons:

> The trend was strong in Biloxi, Miss.; Richmond, Va., and Rockport, Mass.

Colon

5.18   A colon may be used to introduce quoted material:

> The President said: "No comment."

A colon may introduce a short or long passage either in or out of quotation marks:

> The following article was cabled from Madrid:
>
> Text of Filbert's address follows:

A colon may introduce a series:

> The U.S. faces two pressing problems: Unemployment and galloping inflation.

A colon may separate the clauses of a compound sentence when the second clause is an illustration, explanation or restatement of the first:

> Filbert had a drawback: He could not win the golf vote.

5.19   **Capitalize** the first word after a colon.

> He had one big trouble: He hesitated.
>
> He had one big trouble: Hesitation.

Dash

5.20   Dashes are used in a variety of ways as substitutes for commas, parentheses, colons and brackets. They are more spectacular than commas and therefore more arresting, but as compared with parentheses and brackets they cause less interruption in the flow of copy. As punctuation to introduce a collection of material, they appear more sweeping and less specific than colons. An em dash is the dash common in running copy.

Uses of the dash:

5.21   **A parenthetical expression**—thrown in as explanation or to give additional detail—may be enclosed in dashes.

5.22   **Introduction of a series** may be accomplished with a dash:

> This year's race is among three Southern candidates—Filbert, Brown and Easterman.

5.23   **Introduction of a section** or entire article may be made with a dash. It is especially useful to substitute a dash for a colon if the section to follow will itself have sentences or subsections introduced by colons.

> Here are reactions around the country—
>
> A pipefitter in a Midwestern town: "I think . . .

5.24   **Emphasis** can be obtained by using a dash before a final word, phrase or clause:

> One thing he wanted more than any other—to be President.
>
> He wanted to win the Presidency—and he won it.

5.25   **An interrupted quotation** may be terminated with a dash:

> *What is your greatest ambition, Senator?*
>
> As to what I want—
>
> *I mean politically, not personally.*

But note that a quote which just trails off should end with three dots:

> "I might run," he said, "if . . . "

5.26   CAUTION. Since the dash is more impressive typographically than the comma, and a more commanding stop, overuse of dashes is even worse than overuse of commas. One dash or pair of dashes is enough for a paragraph, and use in successive paragraphs is often too much. Too many dashes in a single sentence can lead to confusion:

> Filbert—the Republican candidate—if he wins in Nebraska—will be a cinch to go all the way.

Just where the thrown-in matter in that sentence begins and ends is for the reader to puzzle out.

> Those are the major necessities he sees—bigger warheads and a new fleet—which is long overdue.

The dashes read like a pair, but they are not.

An en dash, shorter than an em dash but longer than a hyphen, may be substituted for a hyphen in some cases for clarity. See 5.54.

Period

5.27 A sentence ends with a period unless it ends with something else, like a question mark or an exclamation point. A period is placed after an abbreviation, unless the abbreviation uses an apostrophe or no punctuation at all. (See Chapter 3, "Abbreviations.") A period serves as a decimal point (115.7, $23.52).

5.28 **Abbreviation of a name** by means of a single letter calls for a period:

K. (for King)   A. (for Adams)

But do not use periods after letters that are mere designations not standing for actual names:

A said to B   the X group accused the Y organization

Do not quote or use periods with school grades—A, B, F

5.29 **A quote that trails off** may be ended with three periods:

"Oh, if only . . . "

This is distinct from an interrupted quote, which uses a dash.

Deletions

5.30 **In text matter,** in or out of quotation marks, deletions are treated as follows:

The law states: "He shall be hanged . . . till dead."

Three periods showing deletion are used in addition to any other normal and needed punctuation. If a period is already there, the result will be four periods. Example before and after deletion:

"That was the end of the case. Nothing more followed. Sentencing came on Tuesday."

"That was the end of the case. . . . Sentencing came on Tuesday."

5.31 **If you break off a sentence** before the end, do not supply a period, because that would give the impression that the complete original sentence is shown. Use only the three dots:

"That was the end . . . Sentencing came on Tuesday."

5.32 **At the end or beginning** of a paragraph, deletions from textual or quoted matter follow the same rules as internally. Before and after deletions:

> BEFORE: He went to the bar to see if she was still there. But he couldn't find anybody.
>
> The next day, Tuesday, he asked about her at the neighbors'.
>
> AFTER: He went to the bar to see if she was still there. But . . .
>
> . . . Tuesday, he asked about her at the neighbors'.

5.33 **Retain the original punctuation** before or after a deletion only if necessary to the sense of the sentence. Before and after:

> "To sharpen the knife, you must use a stone."
>
> "To sharpen the knife . . . use a stone."
>
> "Observe these herbs: thyme, rosemary and oregano."
>
> "Observe these herbs: . . . rosemary and oregano."

5.34 **Where paragraphs are omitted,** we no longer use asterisks. Three dots are added at the end of the last paragraph before the deletion. If in addition to eliminating paragraphs you delete the beginning of the paragraph following the deletion, dots should be placed at the beginning of that paragraph too.

Quotation Marks

5.35 **Statements** or other wording quoted verbatim from an informant, speaker, document, book, magazine article or similar source are enclosed in quotation marks. Do not place marks around material that has been paraphrased, or altered in any other way except by deletions indicated with dots or by explanatory matter inserted between brackets. Complete texts or lengthy excerpts appearing as separate features or boxes sometimes go without quotation marks, but must be properly introduced to make their origin clear. Interviews are not in quotation marks.

5.36 **Paragraphing of quotations** is a matter for choice. Former rules to the contrary having been abolished, a quote may be introduced, begin and continue for an indefinite number of sentences in the same paragraph:

Filbert declared: "I am not a candidate. I have never been a candidate. And if xxx

5.37   **Partial sentences** beginning a quote may lead directly into a continuation of the quote:

Brown said that the building "is a monstrosity. It should be torn down and replaced."

5.38   **Punctuation** should be placed as follows with relation to quotation marks—

Commas and periods should always come before a final quote, not after, even if they have nothing to do with the matter quoted:

Senator Brown said he had not seen "Happiness in Eden," but Filbert has seen it twice.

Senator Genevieve Sullivan still votes with Senator Filbert, even though she has referred to him as a "bunco artist."

Exclamation marks, question marks, semicolons and colons are placed inside of quotation marks when part of the quotation; otherwise outside:

One question the President kept asking himself: Who were these "cronies"?

He demanded, "Who are they?"

Filbert used the slogan "Jail the thieves"; but he would not say who the culprits were.

Filbert attacked "muggers, for their cruelty; burglars, for their stealth;" and various other criminal groups.

He had this to say about "sly embezzlers": They slink.

He declaimed: "I'll tell you this about embezzlers:" but there he stopped.

5.39   **Titles** of plays, movies, operas, radio and TV programs, short stories, articles, individual poems (except book-length poems), speeches, small pamphlets and chapters are in quotes.

5.40   **Names of musical compositions** are quoted when they contain words other than technical terms. Confine the marks to such words:

Mozart's Symphony No. 41 in C Major

Mozart's "Jupiter" Symphony   Schubert's Eighth Symphony

MacDowell's "To a Wild Rose"   Grieg's Piano Concerto in A Minor

(NOTE: Names of newspapers, magazines and books are italicized. See 5.55-5.57.)

5.41   **Political terms** that have achieved historic significance or
familiarity are NOT put in quotation marks:

New Deal   Bull Moose   Great Society   New Frontier

Care should be taken to assure understanding. If the
context does not serve, then:

the Bull Moose campaign of Teddy Roosevelt

Lyndon Johnson's Great Society

Quotes on new or obscure movements or campaign slo-
gans will have to depend upon a judgment of general recognition.

5.42   *Liberal* and *conservative,* as designations of a person's political faith, are not quoted. Since these terms often reflect the
writer's individual judgment and may not correspond to
another writer's interpretation or a reader's, it is best to
reserve them for cases on which there is widespread agreement. Often it is feasible to be more specific:

Senator Filbert, who usually has voted with the spenders, . . .

General Grusam, a former Nazi, . . .

5.43   **Slang** and other nonstandard words do not ordinarily require
quotation marks except when we attribute them, directly or
by implication, to persons or groups (see Chapter 16).

5.44   **A pat word or phrase** that serves as the name of an object or
idea for discussion may usefully be put in quotation marks:

"Urban guerrillas" are a loose conglomeration, sometimes
deadly, sometimes hardly more than a threatening
phrase.

Use of quotation marks in such a case involves a delicate
shade of meaning. If we are speaking of substance rather than
language, no punctuation need be used:

Urban guerrillas are dangerous.

Or if the phrase is offered directly for definition, it may be
italicized:

Urban guerrillas is a name given to groups organized for
sabotage and killing in the cities.

5.45 **Nicknames** are quoted the first time they appear in a given article; use of parentheses is discontinued:

David "Greasy Foot" Filbert

If for some reason a person with a very familiar nickname appears for the first time with the nickname only, quotes need not be used: Ted Kennedy, Jerry Brown. Do not quote nicknames on subsequent use unless there is danger of offense.

5.46 **Fanciful names of aircraft,** if given to individual planes, are put in quotation marks:

"Spirit of St. Louis"   "Air Force One"

Fanciful names of aircraft models or types are capitalized but not quoted:

Lockheed Constellation   McDonnell Phantom

5.47 **Names of buildings and private homes** are NOT quoted:

the Empire State Building   his home, Marmion

5.48 *Yes* and *No* may be attributed to speakers in two ways:

She said yes.   He said no.

She said "Yes."   He said "No."

Hyphen

5.49 Hyphens are used in many types of word combinations. For details, see Chapter 17, "Compound Words."

5.50 **Multiple modifiers,** when merely strung together to serve as adjectives for an immediate purpose, without intent to form a new word, are usually hyphenated:

workers'-compensation laws

citizens'-band radio

a pay-as-you-play policy

If the combination is in quotation marks, no hyphens:

a "pay as you play" saxophone

But if the combination is part of a larger quote, hyphens remain:

He called his music store a "pay-as-you-play emporium."

5.51 **X-to-Y combinations** such as *15-to-20-year-olds* carry hyphens all the way. If these become too complicated, they can be expressed in some other manner:

persons 15 to 20 years old

5.52 **In compound numbers** from twenty-one to ninety-nine, when spelled out (as at the beginning of a sentence) hyphens should be used.

5.53 **Fractions** should not be hyphenated when used as nouns, but are hyphenated when used in the adjective form.

two thirds of his fortune   a two-thirds increase

5.54 **Misleading hyphens** such as those below should be avoided if possible by rewriting, but this cannot always be done:

Big Stone Gap-Clifton Forge area   New York-great circle route

white-collar-blue-collar contrast   anti-Colonial Dames attitude

If it is considered essential to clarify one of these expressions, an en dash may be substituted for the offending hyphen. The en dash is longer than a hyphen but shorter than the em dash normal in running copy:

Big Stone Gap–Clifton Forge area   New York–great-circle route

white-collar–blue-collar contrast   anti–Colonial Dames attitude

If this expedient is used it will have to be styled in by the Desk, unless the writer is working at a computer keyboard or wishes to indicate it on copy.

Italics

5.55 **Names of newspapers, magazines** and similar periodicals are italicized. Do not capitalize or italicize "the" in such names. Italicize the name of the city in names of all newspapers. Capitalize and italicize "Magazine" only if the word is part of the title.

the *New York Times;* the *Times*

the *Lexington Herald*   the *Lexington* (Ky.) *Herald*

Harper's Magazine   the *Atlantic Monthly*

Time or *Time* magazine   the *Federal Register*

U.S.News & World Report; USN&WR

5.56 In credit lines for photos and cartoons, omit "the" from names of newspapers and magazines:

FILBERT—*NEW YORK TIMES*

MacNELLY IN *RICHMOND NEWS LEADER*

5.57 **Names of books,** including book-length poems, are italicized. But do not italicize or quote names of standard dictionaries and encyclopedias or of religious books like the Bible and the Koran.

(NOTE: For other types of publications, see 5.39 and 5.40 in the section on quotation marks, this chapter.)

5.58 **Foreign words,** if so designated by a dictionary that gives this guidance—such as Webster's New World—are to be italicized. If you use words not in the dictionary but known to you as foreign, italicize those too.

5.59 **Names of ships** are italicized:

the U.S.S. *Enterprise*

5.60 **A word referred to as a word only,** not used for its meaning, is italicized:

He inserted an *and* in the record.

5.61 **Legal citations** are italicized:

Haley v. Oklahoma

Apostrophe

5.62 **Possessives of singular words** normally are formed by addition of *'s*:

a man's home   James's friend

Exception: If a word ends in two successive *s* or *z* sounds, only an apostrophe is used to form the possessive:

Moses' tablets   Jesus' parables

CAUTION: For Mr. Bessels, the possessive is Mr. Bessels', not (mistake sometimes made) Mr. *Bessel's*.

5.63 **In some set expressions,** especially before the word *sake*, only an apostrophe is used to form the possessive:

    for goodness' sake   for convenience' sake

5.64 **Ancient classical names** ending in *s* take only the apostrophe to form the possessive:

    Achilles' heel   Pericles' head

5.65 **Possessives of plural words** that have become plural by addition of *s* or *es* are formed by an apostrophe only:

    leaders' views   the Joneses' house

    CAUTION: Not (mistake sometimes made) *the Jone's house* or *the Jones' house*

5.66 Possessives of italicized words are monsters and should be avoided, if possible, by writing around them. But if you must use one, italicize the *s*:

    the *Times's* opinion

5.67 **For plural of letters,** use *'s*:

    4-F's   GI's

5.68 **For plural of numbers,** add only *s*:

    F-16s   1970s   the '30s

5.69 **In plurals of proper names,** do not use apostrophe or alter spelling:

    all the Marys   two Germanys   1977 Oldsmobiles

5.70 **Before *Union*** in union names, except where the word before *Union* ends with *-men*, omit apostrophe:

    Chemical Workers Union

    International Longshoremen's Union

    BUT: International Ladies' Garment Workers Union

5.71 **In the name of a company,** association or governmental agency, if the official and verifiable name omits an apostrophe, so do we:

    Veterans Administration

5.72   **In gerund constructions,** an apostrophe is grammatically required:

> The Secret Service would not hear of the President's going out alone.

A test of this construction: You would not write: "I will not hear of him going out alone." You would write: "I will not hear of his going out alone."

But when the language becomes unbearably complicated, the apostrophe is dropped:

> There is no chance of John's winning appointment.

> There is no chance of John, Mary and Elmira winning appointment.

5.73   **In *a friend of . . . a book of . . .*** and similar expressions, but only in the singular, a double possessive is used:

> A friend of the President's   a book of the professor's

Test of this construction: You would not say, "He was a friend of me."

5.74   **For travel time,** use a hyphen construction or an apostrophe construction, but do not mix them:

> RIGHT: a 2-hour flight
>   a 2 hours' flight
>
> WRONG: a 2-hours' flight

Parentheses

5.75   **Explanatory matter** thrown into a sentence or paragraph often is placed in parentheses. For straight news copy, however, this device is seldom used; it looks unnecessarily academic and precious.

Not recommended:

> Coolidge stayed there (although it was only for an hour) and listened to his Secretary of State.

Recommended:

> Coolidge stayed there—although it was only for an hour—and listened to his Secretary of State.

5.76   **References** from within an article to a chart or box or another article are usually placed in parentheses:

> Gains were unevenly scattered (see chart on page 56).

5.77   **Terminal periods** are placed outside a parenthesis at the end of a sentence if the inserted matter is part of a larger sentence, inside if the matter stands independently:

> Mr. Filbert denied all the charges (for his exact words, see interview on page 73).

> Construction forged ahead in Iowa. Boat sales were up in Rhode Island. Shuffleboard equipment did well in Florida. (A region-by-region survey appears on page 107.)

Brackets

5.78   **Explanatory matter** inserted by us in exact texts or quoted passages should be enclosed in brackets:

> "He stayed through the last meeting [March 26, 1977] before flying home."

Accent Marks

5.79   **Accents used** in *USN&WR* are these:

acute: Perón	grave: Sainte-Geneviève-des-Bois
circumflex: château	tilde: São Paulo
cedilla: Curaçao	umlaut: Kurfürstendamm, naïve

e for umlaut—for example, Duesseldorf instead of Düsseldorf—is a style followed primarily by publications that do not use accents. Since we do use accents, we do not substitute the *e*. However, since some names actually do use *ae*, *oe* and *ue* combinations, we always have to be aware of the right spelling. Correspondents should be requested to avoid spelling *ä* as *ae*, and so on, but to indicate the umlaut in some way. Also, if a person really is named Schoenhaus, not Schönhaus, for example, they should confirm.

Less familiar accents such as the Scandinavian, Czech and Hungarian are not used in *USN&WR*.

In headlines, captions, etc., except for all-cap lines and

NOTES

FIGURES

6.0 In general, spell out both cardinal and ordinal numbers below 10 (weights, measures, ages, and hours, minutes and seconds are among the exceptions). Use numerals for numbers 10 and up.

nine salesmen	the eighth door
10 hammers	the 10th year

Ages

6.1 Use figures for all ages:

a 6-year-old boy   a man in his 40s

when Axel Rodman was 6 years old
Mary Doe, 43, jumped from the deck

Automobiles

6.2

a two-door sedan	the car has six cylinders
a six-cylinder engine	a V-8 engine

Beginning a Sentence

6.3 Spell out numbers beginning a sentence except when figures are used to denote numbered sentences or paragraphs:

Forty-three marines landed in the first wave.

Four million dollars was spent on the breakwater.

Nineteen seventy-four was a good year.

1. Neither party shall break the peace without notice.

It is not necessary to spell out a number after a colon unless what follows the colon is a complete sentence:

Result of his speech: Forty million voters switched.

Switched by his speech: 40 million voters.

Dividing Between Lines

6.4 Do not divide a figure at the end of a line if there is any alternative, even rewriting. If a split is made, it should come after a comma:

350,437,-
402

Fractions

6.5 Spell out fractions, such as *one half, one fourth,* when not part of a larger figure. When spelling out, hyphenate fraction used as an adjective; do not use hyphen when fraction is used as a noun. When a fraction is added to a number, use figures for the entire number.

2½ percent   one-half destroyed   one half of the total

He bought two bearskins, 2½ bolts of cloth.

When adding a fraction to a complete number, if the fraction is other than ½ or ¼, write it as follows, with a space and a slash mark: 6 7/8. The printing operation will close up the space and reduce the fraction to proper size.

Headlines

6.6 Figures may be used in headlines, if desired, for numbers of any size:

THE 5 LIVES OF HENRY THE KATT

If figures are used for one or more numbers under 10 in any given headline, figures must be used for all such numbers in that headline:

WRONG: **Seven Ships in the Canal, 5 at Sea**

Lists, Enumerations

6.7 In lists and enumerations, treat alike all numbers of a group's elements:

First, the Celts. Second, the Saxons. Third, the Normans.

1. The United States did not sign the treaty.
2. Congress acted without responsibility.

These were the steps that led to war: (1) Establishment of the base at Bara Neva; (2) issuance of the U.S. ultimatum; (3) rejection of the ultimatum.

Military

6.8 Numerical designations of military units follow the general rules for numbers:

Sixth Fleet   45th Division   First Corps

Million, Billion, Trillion

6.9 When using numbers in millions, billions or trillions, substitute the word for the ciphers. Portions of a million, billion or trillion may be shown in decimals but, except where necessary to show fine distinctions, round to no more than one digit after the decimal point.

8 million   2.3 billion   1.5 trillion

If vital to go beyond one digit, up to three may be used. If exact numbers must be carried still further to show the desired information, use figures all the way:

8,737,542   7,346,507,000

Use *million* or *billion,* singular, to express numbers of dollars so long as dollars are plainly understood. Repeat *dollars* when necessary for understanding. Do not use the plural *millions* or *billions* except in special cases.

spending 50 billion for aid   millions were wasted

Money

6.10 Use figures for sums of money. Foreign currency should be changed to equivalent in U.S. dollars where possible.

at $3 per 200 pounds   2.5 billion dollars

20 million dollars   75 cents apiece

Sums of money ordinarily are treated as singular:

Thirty billion dollars was appropriated.

In all, 50 million was stolen.

BUT: Millions of dollars were spirited away.

Percentages

6.11 Percentages generally are expressed in figures. Use % mark in tabular matter or headlines if necessary, and in newsletter-type pages where desired.

> Interest was promised at 3 percent.
>
> Prices chalked up an 8 percent increase.
>
> Unemployment declined only one half of 1 percent.
>
> Eighty-one percent of those replying favored Filbert.

Plurals of Numbers

6.12 Form plurals of numbers by adding only *s:*

> B-52s   1940s   the '30s

Roman Numerals

6.13 Use Roman numerals to designate kings and popes; ships, automobiles and machines that incorporate such numerals into their names; sections of documents where so styled by the issuers or desired by the authors; for "The Second" in names of individuals; and for other, similar purposes as indicated by copy at hand:

> Pope Pius XII   the *Laughing Lass II*
>
> George III   II. The parties shall establish . . .
>
> a Lincoln Mark IV   IV. Income and Outgo
>
> Samuel Belvidere II

Scores, Vote Tabulation, Ratios

6.14 Figures are used in a variety of situations involving scores and comparisons:

> The Blue Sox won, 5 to 3.
>
> It was Jones 324, Heffner 213, Smith 2.
>
> Final vote: 15 for, 3 against.
>
> In Indiana, 2 out of 3 disapprove.
>
> The motion passed, 7 to 2.

Series, Statistical Articles

6.15   Whenever numbers are thickly clustered in a series, paragraph or entire article, figures may be used.

In a sentence, three numerical items in a series are enough to call for figures:

> She bought 7 shares of AT&T, 3 of GM and 20 of United Aircraft.

In a paragraph, a large concentration of related numbers may be expressed in figures.

In an article, if related numbers appear repeatedly and in large quantity, figures may be used. Especially subject to this need are political surveys of the sort that detail the numbers of electoral votes a candidate will win by region or state, or the numbers of seats a party can hope to pick up. A switch to figures in such cases is a matter of judgment.

Stocks and Bonds

6.16   Use figures to indicate types of stocks and bonds:

> sale of 2½s increased   3 percent bonds

Temperature

6.17   Use figures to indicate number of degrees. Except in tabular matter or series, spell out *degrees* and the designation of the scale being used. In tables or series, abbreviations may be used.

> 7 degrees below zero Fahrenheit (abbreviation: $-7\,°F$)
>
> between 5 and 6 degrees Celsius (abbreviation: $5°$ to $6°C$)

Time of Day and Dates

6.18   Always use figures for clock time. When using *a.m.* or *p.m.*, lower-case letters and write with periods.

6 a.m.	6 o'clock in the morning
June 29, A.D. 1882	January 12
Dec. 7, 1941	the 20th day of March
the first of January, 1977	Fourth of July (holiday)

Use figures for single years, decades, groups of years:

1800s	1803-05
1900-76	the '20s
1920 and 1921	1450-1425 B.C.

BUT: the Roaring Twenties, etc.

Spell out centuries under 10, use figures from 10 up:

the second century B.C.	third century of the Christian Era (if necessary to distinguish)
the 10th century	20th-century economic theory

Weights, Measurements and Time

6.19   Use figures for weights and measures. Use figures for hours, minutes and seconds. Use figures for years, months, weeks or days when combined with the smaller units.

He stood 6 feet 2 inches	4 hours, 3 minutes
3-ounce jar	a 6-footer

a 6-foot-2-inch man

It flew 2 miles in 9 seconds.

The professor spoke for 2 days and 3 hours.

Elapsed time was 1 day, 3 hours and 6 minutes. (a series)

He stayed in China three years.

(For more on weights and measures, including metric, see 3.15 and 3.16.)

NOTES

NOTES

FOREIGN CURRENCIES

7.0   Authorities differ somewhat on formation of plurals for names of currencies. Where there is disagreement, with one source favoring a plural formed by adding –*s,* that form generally has been chosen for this table. In what follows, second word after country name is the plural.

Afghanistan: afghani, afghanis

Albania: lek, leks

Algeria: dinar, dinars

Angola: kwanza, kwanzas

Argentina: peso, pesos

Australia: dollar, dollars

Austria: schilling, schillings
(but: groschen, groschen)

Bahamas: dollar, dollars

Bahrain: dinar, dinars

Bangladesh: taka, taka

Barbados: dollar, dollars

Belgium: franc, francs

Benin: CFA franc, CFA francs

Bhutan: rupee, rupees

Bolivia: peso, pesos

Botswana: pula, pula

Brazil: cruzeiro, cruzeiros

Bulgaria: lev, leva

Burma: kyat, kyats

Burundi: franc, francs

Cameroon: CFA franc, CFA francs

Canada: dollar, dollars

Cape Verde: escudo, escudos

Cent. African Empire: CFA franc, CFA francs

Chad: CFA franc, CFA francs

Chile: peso, pesos

China, People's Republic of: yuan, yuan

China, Republic of (Taiwan): dollar, dollars

Colombia: peso, pesos

Congo: CFA franc, CFA francs

Costa Rica: colon, colons

Cyprus: pound, pounds

Czechoslovakia: koruna, korunas

Denmark: krone, kroner

Dominican Republic: peso, pesos

East Germany: mark, marks

Ecuador: sucre, sucres

Egypt: pound, pounds

El Salvador: colon, colons

Equatorial Guinea: ekuele, ekueles

Ethiopia: birr, birr

Fiji: dollar, dollars

Finland: markka, markkaa

France: franc, francs

Gabon: CFA franc, CFA francs

Gambia: dalasi, dalasi

Ghana: cedi, cedis

Greece: drachma, drachmas

Grenada: dollar, dollars

Guatemala: quetzal, quetzals

Guinea: syli, sylis

Guinea-Bissau: escudo, escudos

Guyana: dollar, dollars

Haiti: gourde, gourdes

Honduras: lempira, lempiras

Hungary: forint, forints

Iceland: krona, kronur

India: rupee, rupees

Indonesia: rupiah, rupiahs

Iran: rial, rials

Iraq: dinar, dinars

Ireland: pound, pounds

Israel: shekel, shekels

Italy: lira, lire

Ivory Coast: CFA franc, CFA francs

Jamaica: dollar, dollars

Japan: yen, yen

Jordan: dinar, dinars

Kenya: shilling, shillings

Korea (North and South): won, won

Kuwait: dinar, dinars

Laos: kip, kips

Lebanon: pound, pounds

Lesotho: rand, rands

Liberia: dollar, dollars

Libya: dinar, dinars

Liechtenstein: franc, francs

Luxembourg: franc, francs

Madagascar: franc, francs

Malawi: kwacha, kwacha

Malaysia: ringgit, ringgits

Maldives: rupee, rupees

Mali: franc, francs

Malta: pound, pounds

Mauritania: ouguiya, ouguiyas

Mauritius: rupee, rupees

Mexico: peso, pesos

Monaco: franc, francs

Mongolia: tugrik, tugriks

Morocco: dirham, dirhams

Mozambique: escudo, escudos

Nepal: rupee, rupees

Netherlands: guilder, guilders
   (in Dutch language: gulden, gulden)

New Zealand: dollar, dollars

Nicaragua: cordoba, cordobas

Niger: CFA franc, CFA francs

Nigeria: naira, naira

Norway: krone, kroner

Oman: rial, rials

Pakistan: rupee, rupees

Panama: balboa, balboas

Papua New Guinea: kina, kina

Paraguay: guarani, guaranis

Peru: sol, soles

Philippines: peso, pesos

Poland: zloty, zlotys

Portugal: escudo, escudos

Qatar: riyal, riyals

Rumania: leu, lei

Rwanda: franc, francs

Samoa, Western: tala, talas

São Tomé and Príncipe: escudo, escudos

Saudi Arabia: riyal, riyals

Senegal: CFA franc, CFA francs

Seychelles: rupee, rupees

Sierra Leone: leone, leones

Singapore: dollar, dollars

Somalia: shilling, shillings

South Africa: rand, rands

Spain: peseta, pesetas

Sri Lanka: rupee, rupees

Sudan: pound, pounds

Suriname: guilder, guilders

Swaziland: lilangeni, emalangeni

Sweden: krona, kronor

Switzerland: franc, francs

Syria: pound, pounds

Tanzania: shilling, shillings

Thailand: baht, bahts

Togo: CFA franc, CFA francs

Transkei: rand, rands

Trinidad: dollar, dollars

Tunisia: dinar, dinars

Turkey: lira, liras

Uganda: shilling, shillings

United Arab Emirates: dirham, dirhams

United Kingdom: pound, pounds

Upper Volta: CFA franc, CFA francs

Uruguay: peso, pesos

U.S.S.R.: ruble, rubles

Venezuela: bolivar, bolivars

Vietnam: dong, dong

West Germany: deutsche mark, deutsche marks,
    but usually mark, marks

Yemen, North: rial, rials
    (Yemen Arab Republic)

Yemen, South: dinar, dinars
    (People's Democratic Republic of Yemen)

Yugoslavia: dinar, dinars

Zaire: zaire, zaires

Zambia: kwacha, kwacha

7.1   **Information** about the world's currencies is kept up to date by three periodicals: *International Financial Statistics,* published monthly by the International Monetary Fund; *Monthly Bulletin of Statistics,* from the United Nations, and *Statistical Release H-10,* weekly from the Federal Reserve Board.

NAMES OF PERSONS

8.0   A name is the appellation a person received at birth or adopted legally or took informally for professional purposes, such as a stage name or pen name. Treatment of the name under various circumstances may require a choice of style.

8.1   **Help with names.** Sources of information about names are Webster's New World Dictionary, the biographical section of Merriam-Webster's New Collegiate Dictionary, and Merriam-Webster's Biographical Dictionary. Further assistance, including a chance to see how particular names are used, is in *Current Biography* and the encyclopedias, Britannica and Americana. With foreign names, aid can be had from the country desks of the State Department; from the State Department's Diplomatic List; from *Chiefs of State and Cabinet Members of Foreign Countries,* published by the CIA. In using these sources, however, try to apply our own rules—if any— for the country in question. Special sources for some particular countries are mentioned in what follows.

8.2   **Foreign-origin names.** Citizens of English-speaking countries often bear names, of foreign origin, that begin with the particles *de, du, da, von, van,* etc. These particles are likely to be capitalized in Anglicized names, but this is not always the case. On subsequent reference the particle usually is capitalized or lower-cased as in the full name:

Paul de Kruif; a de Kruif book	Eamon de Valera; in de Valera's time
Lee De Forest; the De Forest genius	James A. Van Allen; the Van Allen belt

A particle starting a sentence or headline is capitalized.

8.3   **Du Pont.** This name takes various forms in different branches of the family. It also is handled in an unusual manner in the company's name, which is E. I. du Pont de Nemours & Company when full but the Du Pont Company or Du Pont when only the surname is used.

8.4   **Nicknames.** See 5.45 in "Punctuation."

Mr., Mrs., Miss, Ms.

8.5   *Mr.* is not used either on first or on subsequent mention with men's names:

> James Jones; Jones
>
> the Rev. John Doe; Doe

Mrs., Miss, Ms. are not used with women's names:

> Jane Roe; Roe
>
> the Rev. Mary Doe; Doe

Mr., Mrs., Miss or *Ms.* may always be used for purposes of clarity, or when a point is being made of the marital relationship, or when a purely domestic situation is being described:

> Jane and Jerry Jessup differ in their voting plans. Mrs. Jessup is backing Snyder, but Mr. Jessup is for Beasley.

Mr., Mrs., etc., may also be used in forms of address:

> Good luck, Mr. Carter.
>
> Dear Mrs. Green:

The above rules for *Mr., Mrs.,* etc., do not apply to quoted material, texts or interviews.

Foreign Names

8.6   **Particles.** When affixed to foreign names, particles *da, de, della, des, do, du, la, l', ten, ter, van* and *von* often imply family distinction. Press practice has varied widely on keeping or dropping the particle when the surname stands alone. Since some authorities and many individuals object strongly to dropping the particle, the only safe course is to repeat it unless you know that the individual customarily drops it. Keeping it is seldom incorrect in modern names.

A particle repeated in a foreign surname standing alone should be capitalized or lower-cased just as it appears in the full name:

Charles de Gaulle; de Gaulle   Ferdinand de Lesseps; de Lesseps

Francois de La Gorce; La Gorce

Historic names should be used in their familiar forms for the sake of recognition:

Wolfgang von Goethe; Goethe   Hernando De Soto; De Soto

Vincent van Gogh; van Gogh   Tomas de Torquemada; Torquemada

When a particle starts a sentence, it is capitalized.

8.7   **Arabs' names.** Two kinds of confusion arise in treating Arabs' names: first, over spelling; second, over what parts of a name to use, especially on subsequent mention.

SPELLING is standardized in Arabic script. Variations grew out of Western efforts to reproduce Arabic sounds: A French administrator might spell a name with an *-oun* or an American reporter with a *-un* or a *-ur,* depending on his ear and education.

In this process, some much-used Arabic names have acquired generally accepted spellings, which will continue to be followed. Also, a number of Arabs are westernizing their names in a variety of ways; their preferences should be honored.

Where neither a personal preference nor an agreed spelling exists, writers and editors have recourse to the standardized, letter-by-letter system of transliteration devised by the Library of Congress. Books kept at the Name Checker's desk in the *USN&WR* newsroom supply the standard spellings of nearly all names and parts of names that Arabs use. Ignore the apostrophelike marks and the hyphens before *al.*

FORMS of Arabic names have confused the Western press simply because they do not usually consist of Western-type given, middle and family names. The last word in the name may be, as in the case of Nasser, just a part of the father's name, or it may be, as with Qadhafi, a reference to the individual's native town, or it may be a nickname describing an occupation or a physical peculiarity. Nevertheless, standard press procedure in most cases is to use only the last word of a name in subsequent references.

Saudi princes, however, are known by their first names: Prince Fahd ibn Abdel-Aziz; Prince Fahd; Fahd.

An understanding of form may be helpful. For example:

Gamal Abdel Nasser; Nasser

Nasser's name was formed as follows:

Gamal (the individual's name)

Abd al-Nasir (father's name)

Abd al-Nasir breaks down this way:

Abd (worshiper of)

al (the)

Nasir (Victorious One—one of the names of God)

Sometimes a grandfather's name is added, and sometimes a family name, too. Sometimes a particle meaning *son of* or *daughter of* is inserted before the father's name and the grandfather's name:

ibn, bin, ben: son of; *bint:* daughter of

Spell it *ibn* unless another spelling is firmly established. Lower-case when preceded by other parts of the name; capitalize when it is the first part used, as in Ibn Saud.

Other parts used in putting names together:

al, el, ed, as, ud, ul, ur: the

Unless hard sources or individual preference dictate otherwise, spell it *al* and hyphenate to the following word. Drop it on second reference.

Abu: father of; used in various combinations

Abd: worshiper of

Allah, Ullah: primary name of God

Abd and Allah combine in diverse forms such as Abdulla, worshiper of God; Ala al-Din, God of the religion; Nasr Allah (sometimes Nasrullah), victory of God.

8.8   WOMEN'S NAMES in Arab countries sometimes are formed by adding *a* to masculine names, as in Hasana, from Hasan (but an *a* ending does not necessarily mean a feminine name, as some men's names also end in *a*.) Many others are primarily feminine, such as Lala (tulip), Jabra (lamb), Yasimun (jasmine), Zahra (flower).

Zahra, daughter of Sulaiman, would probably be known as

Zahra bint Sulaiman. If she marries Ali Muhammad she will be known as Zahra marat Ali, or more completely, Zahra bint Sulaiman marat Ali Muhammad. Or *zawiat* might be substituted for *marat.*

In the American press and in American society, however, Zahra would be known as Mrs. Muhammad, or, more fully, Mrs. Ali Muhammad.

8.9 GENERAL RULES, therefore, for names of Arabs:

1. If the individual has westernized his name, use his spelling, and use the name he elects for subsequent mention unless it is too cumbersome.

2. In the absence of known preference, use the established and agreed form and spelling.

3. If there is disagreement about form or spelling, get as close as possible to standard press practice described in this section.

8.10 ESTABLISHED spellings in the *USN&WR* file are as follows. The name before the comma is the one for second reference, except for Prince Fahd:

Adasani, Mahmud
Abdel-Meguid, Adly
Arafat, Yassir
Arif, Abdul Rahman
Assad, Hafez
Attassi, Nureddin
Badran, Madar
Bakr, Ahmed Hassan
Fahmy, Ismail
Prince Fahd ibn
    Abdel-Aziz; Fahd
Hegazi, Abdul Aziz
Ismail, Gen. Ahmed Ali
Jalloud, Abdul Salam
Naguib, Muhammad
Nimeri, Jafar Mohamed
Qadhafi, Muammar
Qusaibi, Ghazi al-
Rafei, Abdul Ghani
Sabah, Sheik Sabah al-Salim al-
Sulaim, Sulaiman al-
Tal, Wasfi
Yaffi, Abdullah
Yamani, Sheik Ahmed Zaki
Zayyat, Mohammed

8.11   HELP WITH QUESTIONS:

An Arabic-speaking writer on the staff

Near East Section, Library of Congress

Foreign Service Institute of the State Department

Country desks of the State Department

Press officers of Arab diplomatic missions

8.12   **Chinese names.** In Chinese names the family name generally comes first. The given name usually is in two parts, hyphenated, with the second part lower-cased:

Chou En-lai; Chou	Peng Teh-huai; Peng
Hua Kuo-feng; Hua	Mao Tse-tung; Mao

Some ancient names consist of only two parts, both of which must be repeated on subsequent reference:

Li Po	Lao-tzu

A few modern names have only two elements:

Chi Liu; Liu

Chiang Ching; to be correct, repeat both names on subsequent mention.

Some Chinese, especially those educated in the West, have westernized their names, putting the family name last. Usually, but not always, this is done in such a way that the family and given names are easy to tell apart:

Stephen Soo-ming Lo; Lo	James C. H. Shen; Shen
Ha-hsiung Wen; Wen	Yu Sung; Sung

8.13   **French names.** Spelling and capitalization follow the individual's style, and retain that style on subsequent mention.

8.14   *La, Le, Les* usually are capitalized:

Maurice de La Gorce; the La Gorce story; La Gorce

Des, Du usually are capitalized if they occur at the start of a surname:

Pierre Du Pre; Du Pre	Armand Dupre; Dupre

BUT watch out for double surnames. They raise questions not only of capitalization but of recognition; you have to be sure you do not mistake the first half of a double surname for a given name. An interior particle is likely to be lower-cased:

Bernard Reynold du Chaffaut; Reynold du Chaffaut

de or the contraction *d'* is usually lower-cased.

8.15 **German names.** Use the diphthong *ae, ie, oe* or *ue* only if you know that to be the way the individual spells his name; if he uses an umlaut and it is available in your mechanical system, use the umlaut, do not substitute the extra *e:*

> Wolfgang von Goethe (that's the way it's spelled)
>
> Erich Spätmann (if he spells it that way; NOT Spaetmann)

8.16 **Portuguese names.** By Portuguese statement, "Portuguese do about as they please" in the use of their names.

Some surnames are single, as in Luis Martins. Some are double, as in Albino Cabral Pessoa.

Double surnames put the mother's name first and the father's second. Thus if one surname is used in subsequent mention of a person, it should be the last surname. Be sure you are referring to a Portuguese, not a Spaniard; Spanish surnames place the mother's last, and it is a faux pas to use the mother's name alone.

Most Portuguese repeat only one surname, but a few choose to repeat both if they have two:

Luis Martins; Martins   João Hall Themido; Themido

Roque Felix Dias; Felix Dias

In any case of doubt, it is safe to repeat both parts of a double surname.

8.17 A WOMAN'S NAME before marriage follows the same patterns as a man's. But if Maria Soares marries Ruy Cordeiro, she almost always becomes Maria Soares Cordeiro; Mrs. Ruy Cordeiro; Cordeiro or Mrs. Cordeiro. In Portugal, custom permits a woman on marrying to retain her maiden name: Mrs. Maria Soares.

8.18 **Brazilian names.** Names of Brazilians generally resemble the Portuguese. Even more caution is indicated in determining individual usage, because movement of people in and out of the country mixes types of names. Here, too, it is safe to use both parts of a double surname if there are doubts.

Some illustrative Brazilian names:

> João Baptista Pinheiro; Pinheiro

Francisco Thompson Flores Neto; Thompson Flores (Neto is not a basic part of the name, but an appendage like *Junior*)

Mrs. Maria Regina Breves Barringer; Barringer or Mrs. Barringer

Ms. Loana Braga Barbosa; Barbosa or Ms. Barbosa

8.19   **Russian names.** When these come to a news writer or editor, they usually have been transliterated by any of several systems that produce a variety of results. The Russian original seldom is available, so even the editor with a knowledge of the Cyrillic alphabet cannot check back on spelling. The only way to maintain any uniformity is to follow rules of thumb.

E'S AND ENDINGS. Guides outlined here are based on a transliteration system especially recommended for the press by J. Thomas Shaw, professor of Slavic languages at the University of Wisconsin, and on other authorities—

The Russian *e* can sound like *e* in *pet,* *ye* in *Yehudi,* or *yo* in *yodel.*

When you find the *ye* form at the beginning of a name, retain it; when you do not find it but you know the name ordinarily has it, supply it:

Yevgeny, not Evgeny   Yekaterina, not Ekaterina

Yevtushenko, not Evtushenko

But in the interior of a name, do not use the *ye* form:

Dostoevsky, not Dostoyevsky   Sergeevich, not Sergeyevich

Alexeevich, not Alexeyevich   Andreevich, not Andreyevich

Familiar names that are known to have the *yo* sound for *e* should be spelled that way:

Pyotr, not Petr   Semyon, not Semen   Fyodor, not Fedor

If in the transliteration that comes to you a name is spelled with an ë (*e* with umlaut), treat the word as you would if it were spelled with an ordinary *e:*

Pëtr: Pyotr   Zhigalëv: Zhigalev

In news articles, use *x,* not *ks:*

Alexey, not Aleksey   Alexandr, not Aleksandr

Maxim Gorky, not Maksim

Use the ending *-y* rather than *-i, -iy, -yi, -yj, ii, ij* for prenames and surnames:

Dmitry, not Dmitri or Dmitriy   Grigory, not Grigoriy
Yevgeny, not Yevgeniy   Georgy, not Georgiy
Vasily, not Vasiliy   Arkady, not Arkadiy
Yury, not Yuriy   Sergey, not Sergei
Anatoly, not Anatoliy   Alexey, not Alexei
Vitaly, not Vitaliy   Tolstoy, not Tolstoi
                                Bely, not Belyy

In general, the following endings also are standard for *USN&WR:*

-sky, not *-ski* (*-ski* is Polish)
-ov, not *-off* (*-off* is French)
-ev, not *-eff* (*-eff* is French)

8.20   HELP WITH NAMES. Anyone wishing to understand more about methods of transliteration, including the one used for this section, should consult *The Transliteration of Modern Russian for English-Language Publications,* by J. Thomas Shaw (published by the University of Wisconsin Press). This booklet contains, among other things, a table of Russian letters with Roman-letter equivalents in the various systems. A copy is kept on the Name Checker's desk at *USN&WR.*

Other help:

Chiefs of State and Cabinet Members of Foreign Governments. A copy of this CIA publication is kept on the Name Checker's desk.

Prominent Personalities in the USSR, published by the Scarecrow Press. This book does not follow all the rules laid down in this section, but can be helpful. A copy of the 1968 edition is kept in the *USN&WR* library, along with supplements for several later years. It will no longer be updated, however.

The Slavic-languages section in the shared cataloging division of the Library of Congress. Employes there use a different method from ours, but they understand and can give advice.

8.21   HISTORIC NAMES. If a name has been established in distant or recent history by a spelling that varies from the norm, it retains that spelling:

Khrushchev, not Khrushchyoff
Peter the Great, not Pyotr the Great

8.22 EMIGRES. Persons of Russian stock who have migrated to other countries, and their descendants, adopt spellings that may vary according to the country. These are accepted spellings and should be used. But foreign spellings for Russians still in Russia or temporarily abroad are not necessarily correct.

8.23 FEMININE ENDINGS OF SURNAMES. U.S. custom is to use these if the woman concerned has an independent reputation, otherwise not:

> Viktoria Brezhnev, not Brezhneva
>
> Yekaterina Furtseva, not Furtsev

8.24 FEMININE ENDINGS OF PRENAMES. Use *ia*, not *iya* or *iia*:

Viktoria, not Viktoriya	Lidia, not Lidiya
Ksenia, not Kseniya	Maria, not Marya
Natalia, not Nataliya	Yevdokia, not Yevdokiya
Klavdia, not Klavdiya	

8.25 **Spanish-language names.** The only safe guide to Spanish-language names is the way the individuals use them.

Some surnames are single names:

> Luis Sierra; Sierra

Other surnames are double:

> Ignacio Castro Cano; Castro
>
> Joaquin Prado y Fernandez; Prado y Fernandez or Prado
>
> Adolfo Martinez-Herrero; Martinez-Herrero or Martinez

Most double names are combinations of the father's surname (first) and the mother's (last).

But some double names come from the father alone and are passed from generation to generation. Presence or absence of a hyphen is no clue to this difference.

For example: Mexico's former President, Luis Echeverría Alvarez. His double surname uses his father's first, his mother's last. He was generally known as President Echeverría. But another example:

President José López Portillo. His double surname comes from his father. The President's grandfather took the name López Portillo from his father and mother, and achieved prominence. Since then, the family's surname has been López Portillo. It cannot be divided, so he is known as López Portillo.

Moreover, some insist on repeating the double names for prestige. Use of double surnames when standing alone is more prevalent in Mexico than elsewhere. In the rest of Latin America, repetition of double surnames is being abandoned by many. But individual usage still varies.

Thus the general rules:

1. Use a name as the individual uses it or as it is used in his local environment. The foreign correspondent or domestic reporter should try to determine this.

2. On second reference, repeat double surnames in their entirety unless you know that the individual is satisfied to use the first surname alone.

3. Never use the second half of a Spanish-language surname alone. This is often considered an objectionable thing to do.

CAUTION: Since some people do have single surnames, care is necessary in recognizing these. In a name with a single surname, naturally the last name is the one to be repeated; in a double surname, the last name must not be repeated alone. In Cuba, for instance:

Fidel Castro Ruz; Castro (it's a double surname)

Carlos Rafael Rodriguez; Rodriguez (Rafael not part of surname)

Some persons with surnames in widespread use, such as López, Peréz, Gonzalez and García, simply add an initial for further identification:

Gonzalez D.   García T.

This looks odd in U.S. print, but it should be honored the first time around and it should be repeated if there is a possibility of doubt about which Gonzalez or García is meant.

8.26   WOMEN'S NAMES in Spanish-speaking countries work this way: If Maria Peréz marries a Mr. Gonzalez, she becomes Maria Peréz de Gonzalez; Gonzalez or Mrs. Gonzalez.

NOTES

NATIVES, NATIONALS

Natives or Inhabitants of States

9.0

Alabamian
Alaskan
Arizonan
Arkansan

Californian
Coloradan
Connecticuter
Delawarean
Floridian
Georgian
Hawaiian
Idahoan
Illinoisan
Indianan
Iowan
Kansan
Kentuckian

Louisianian
Mainer
Marylander
Massachusetts resident, native, etc.
Michigander*
Minnesotan
Mississippian
Missourian
Montanan
Nebraskan
Nevadan
New Hampshirite
New Jerseyite
New Mexican
New Yorker
North Carolinian
North Dakotan

Ohioan
Oklahoman
Oregonian
Pennsylvanian

Rhode Islander
South Carolinian
South Dakotan
Tennessean
Texan
Utahan
Vermonter
Virginian
Washingtonian
West Virginian
Wisconsinite
Wyomingite

*BUT: Michiganian or Michigan traits, etc.

Other Areas Controlled by U.S.

Guamanian   Puerto Rican   Samoan
Virgin Islands (use: native of the Virgin Islands)

Natives or Inhabitants of Canadian Provinces

9.1

Albertan

British Columbian

Nova Scotian

Manitoban

New Brunswicker

Ontarian

Newfoundlander (avoid "Newfie"—fighting word to some)

Prince Edward Islander; can be just Islander after complete term or full name of province has once been used

Quebecker, anybody in or from Quebec Province; Québécois (pl same), a French Canadian in or from Quebec Province

Saskatchewanian, rare; usually "she's from Saskatchewan," "people from Saskatchewan," etc.

(For abbreviations of provinces, see 3.6.)

Words Denoting Nationality, Regional Affinity

9.2	Country or region	Noun (plural ending in parens)	Adjective
	Afars and Issas, French Territory of the	Voted independence as of June 27, 1977. See Djibouti, Republic of	
	Afghanistan	Afghan(s)	Afghan
	Albania	Albanian(s)	Albanian
	Algeria	Algerian(s)	Algerian
	American Samoa	Samoan(s)	Samoan
	Andorra	Andorran(s)	Andorran
	Angola	Angolan(s)	Angolan
	Argentina	Argentine(s)	Argentine
	Australia	Australian(s)	Australian
	Austria	Austrian(s)	Austrian
	Bahamas	Bahamian(s)	Bahamian
	Bahrain	Bahraini(s)	Bahraini
	Bangladesh	Bengali(s)	Bengali
	Barbados	Barbadian(s)	Barbadian
	Belgium	Belgian(s)	Belgian
	Benin	Beninese (sing & pl)	Beninese
	Bhutan	Bhutanese (sing & pl)	Bhutanese
	Bolivia	Bolivian(s)	Bolivian
	Botswana (formerly Bechuanaland)	Motswana (sing) Batswana (pl)	Botswanan
	Brazil	Brazilian(s)	Brazilian
	Bulgaria	Bulgarian(s)	Bulgarian
	Burma	Burmese (sing & pl)	Burmese
	Burundi	Burundian(s)	Burundian
	Byelorussia (part of U.S.S.R.)	Byelorussian(s)	Byelorussian

Country or region	Noun (plural ending in parens)	Adjective
Cambodia	Cambodian(s)	Cambodian
Cameroon	Cameroonian(s)	Cameroonian
Canada	Canadian(s)	Canadian
Cape Verde	Cape Verdian(s)	Cape Verdian
Central African Republic	Central African(s)	Central African
Ceylon—now Sri Lanka		
Chad	Chadian(s)	Chadian
Chile	Chilean(s)	Chilean
China, Nationalist or Communist	Chinese (sing & pl)	Chinese

Correct names are:
    People's Republic of China; subsequently China, mainland China, Communist China
    Republic of China (Taiwan); subsequently Taiwan or Nationalist China

Colombia	Colombian(s)	Colombian
Comoros	Comoro(s)	Comoro
Congo (People's Republic of the Congo, formerly Congo-Brazzaville)	Congolese (sing & pl)	Congolese
Congo-Kinshasa, formerly Leopoldville—now Zaire		
Costa Rica	Costa Rican(s)	Costa Rican
Cuba	Cuban(s)	Cuban
Cyprus	Cypriot(s)	Cypriot
Czechoslovakia	Czechoslovak(s)	Czechoslovak
Dahomey—now Benin		
Denmark	Dane(s)	Danish
Djibouti, Republic of	Djiboutian(s)	Djiboutian
Dominica (British associated state)	Dominican(s)	Dominican
Dominican Republic	Dominican(s)	Dominican
East Germany (German Democratic Republic)	East German(s)	East German
Ecuador	Ecuadoran(s)	Ecuadoran

Country or region	Noun (plural ending in parens)	Adjective
Egypt	Egyptian(s)	Egyptian
El Salvador	Salvadoran(s)	Salvadoran
Equatorial Guinea	Equatorial Guinean(s)	Equatorial Guinean
Estonia (absorbed into U.S.S.R.)	Estonian(s)	Estonian
Ethiopia	Ethiopian(s)	Ethiopian
Fiji	Fijian(s)	Fijian
Finland	Finn(s)	Finnish
France	the French; Frenchman (men), Frenchwoman, etc.	French
French Somaliland—see Afars and Issas, Djibouti		
Gabon	Gabonese (sing & pl)	Gabonese
Gambia	Gambian(s)	Gambian
Germany (see West Germany, East Germany)	German(s)	German
Ghana	Ghanaian(s)	Ghanaian
Great Britain	Briton(s), British (collective plural)	British
Greece	Greek(s)	Greek
Grenada	Grenadian(s)	Grenadian
Guatemala	Guatemalan(s)	Guatemalan
Guinea	Guinean(s)	Guinean
Guinea-Bissau (formerly Portuguese Guinea)	Guinean(s)	Guinean
Guyana (formerly British Guiana)	Guyanese (sing & pl)	Guyanese
Haiti	Haitian(s)	Haitian
Honduras	Honduran(s)	Honduran
Hungary	Hungarian(s)	Hungarian
Iceland	Icelander(s)	Icelandic
India	Indian(s)	Indian

Country or region	Noun (plural ending in parens)	Adjective
Indo-China (region)	Indo-Chinese (sing & pl)	Indo-Chinese
Indonesia	Indonesian(s)	Indonesian
Iran	Iranian(s)	Iranian
Iraq	Iraqi(s)	Iraqi
Ireland	Irishman (men), Irish (collective plural), Irishwoman, etc.	Irish
Isle of Man	Manxman (men), Manx (collective plural), Manx-woman, Manx resident	Manx
Israel	Israeli(s)	Israeli
Italy	Italian(s)	Italian
Ivory Coast	Ivoirian(s)	Ivoirian
Jamaica	Jamaican(s)	Jamaican
Japan	Japanese (sing & pl)	Japanese
Jordan	Jordanian(s)	Jordanian
Kashmir	Kashmiri(s)	Kashmiri
Kenya	Kenyan(s)	Kenyan
Korea (see North Korea, South Korea)	Korean(s)	Korean
Kuwait	Kuwaiti(s)	Kuwaiti
Laos	Laotian(s)	Laotian, Lao
Latvia	Latvian(s)	Latvian
Lebanon	Lebanese (sing & pl)	Lebanese
Lesotho (formerly Basutoland)	Mosotho (sing); Basotho (pl)	Basotho
Liberia	Liberian(s)	Liberian
Libya	Libyan(s)	Libyan
Liechtenstein	Liechtensteiner(s)	Liechtenstein
Lithuania (absorbed into U.S.S.R.)	Lithuanian(s)	Lithuanian
Luxembourg	Luxembourger(s)	Luxembourg

Country or region	Noun (plural ending in parens)	Adjective
Macao (Portuguese overseas province)	Macaoan(s)	Macaoan
Madagascar (Democratic Republic of, formerly Malagasy Republic)	Malagasy (sing & pl)	Malagasy (or Madagascan if needed for clarity)
Malawi (formerly Nyasaland)	Malawian(s)	Malawian
Malaysia	Malaysian(s)	Malaysian
Maldives (formerly Maldive Islands)	Maldivian(s)	Maldivian
Mali	Malian(s)	Malian
Malta	Maltese (sing & pl)	Maltese
Mauritania	Mauritanian(s)	Mauritanian
Mauritius	Mauritian(s)	Mauritian
Mexico	Mexican(s)	Mexican
Monaco	Monacan(s)	Monacan
Mongolia	Mongolian(s)	Mongolian
Morocco	Moroccan(s)	Moroccan
Mozambique	Mozambicano(s)	Mozambican
Namibia (formerly South-West Africa)	Namibian(s)	Namibian
Nauru	Nauruan(s)	Nauruan
Nepal	Nepalese (sing & pl)	Nepalese
Netherlands (may be Holland in running copy)	Netherlander(s), Dutchman, Dutchmen, Dutchwoman, Dutchwomen, the Dutch, Hollander(s)	Netherlandish, Dutch; (the Netherlands government or Dutch government)
New Zealand	New Zealander(s)	New Zealand
Newfoundland (Canadian island or province)	Newfoundlander(s)	Newfoundland
Nicaragua	Nicaraguan(s)	Nicaraguan
Niger	Nigerois (sing & pl)	Niger
Nigeria	Nigerian(s)	Nigerian

Country or region	Noun (plural ending in parens)	Adjective
Northern Rhodesia—now Zambia		
Norway	Norwegian(s)	Norwegian
North Korea	North Korean(s)	North Korean
Oman	Omani(s)	Oman, Omani
Pakistan	Pakistani(s)	Pakistani
Palestine	Palestinian(s)	Palestinian
Panama	Panamanian(s)	Panamanian
Papua New Guinea	Papua New Guinean(s)	Papua New Guinean
Paraguay	Paraguayan(s)	Paraguayan
Peru	Peruvian(s)	Peruvian
Philippines	Filipino(s), Filipina(s)	Philippine
Poland	Pole(s)	Polish
Portugal	Portuguese (sing & pl)	Portuguese
Portuguese Guinea— now Guinea-Bissau		
Qatar	Qatari(s)	Qatari
Rhodesia (see Zimbabwe)	Rhodesian(s)	Rhodesian
Rumania	Rumanian(s)	Rumanian
Russia (usable synonym for U.S.S.R. or Soviet Union, but not on maps)	Russian(s) or Soviet citizens	Russian or Soviet
Rwanda (formerly Ruanda-Urundi)	Rwandan(s)	Rwandan
Samoa (see American Samoa, Western Samoa)		
San Marino	San Marinan(s)	San Marinan
São Tomé and Príncipe	São Toméan(s)	São Toméan
Saudi Arabia	Saudi Arab(s)	Saudi Arabian
Scotland	Scot(s), Scotch (collective plural)	Scotch, Scottish

Country or region	Noun (plural ending in parens)	Adjective
Senegal	Senegalese (sing & pl)	Senegalese
Seychelles	Seychellois (sing & pl)	Seychelles
Sierra Leone	Sierra Leonean(s)	Sierra Leonean
Singapore	Singaporean(s)	Singaporean
Somalia	Somali(s)	Somali
South Africa	South African(s)	South African
South Korea	South Korean(s)	South Korean
South-West Africa (see Namibia)		
Soviet Union (U.S.S.R., Russia)	Soviet national(s), Russian(s)	Soviet or Russian
Spain	Spaniard(s)	Spanish
Spanish Sahara (see Western Sahara)		
Sri Lanka (formerly Ceylon)	Ceylonese (sing & pl)	Ceylonese
Sudan	Sudanese (sing & pl)	Sudanese
Suriname	Surinamese (sing & pl)	Surinamese
Swaziland	Swazi(s)	Swaziland
Sweden	Swede(s)	Swedish
Switzerland	Swiss (sing & pl)	Swiss
Syria	Syrian(s)	Syrian
Tanganyika (now a part of Tanzania)	Tanganyikan(s)	Tanganyikan
Tanzania	Tanzanian(s)	Tanzanian
Thailand	Thai (sing & pl)	Thai
Togo	Togolese (sing & pl)	Togolese
Tonga	Tongan(s)	Tongan
Transkei	Transkeian(s)	Transkeian
Trieste	Triestine, Triestini	Triestine

Country or region	Noun (plural ending in parens)	Adjective
Trinidad and Tobago	Trinidadian(s) for inhabitants general- ly; Tobagan(s) for natives of Tobago	Trinidadian, Tobagan
Tunisia	Tunisian(s)	Tunisian
Turkey	Turk(s)	Turkish
Uganda	Ugandan(s)	Ugandan
Ukraine	Ukrainian(s)	Ukrainian
Union of Soviet Socialist Republics (or Soviet Union or Russia)	Soviet national(s) or Soviet citizen(s) or Russian(s)	Soviet or Russian
United Arab Emirates	(Refer to resident of United Arab Emirates or resident of individual Emirate.)	
Abu Dhabi Fujairah Ajman Dubai Ras al-Khaimah Sharjah Umm al-Qaiwain		
United Kingdom (see Great Britain)		
Upper Volta	Upper Voltan(s)	Upper Volta
Uruguay	Uruguayan(s)	Uruguayan
Venezuela	Venezuelan(s)	Venezuelan
Vietnam	Vietnamese (sing & pl)	Vietnamese
Wales	Welshman (men), Welsh (collective plural), Welsh- woman, etc.	Welsh
Western Sahara (temporary designa- tion for former Spanish Sahara)	Western Saharan	Western Saharan(s)
Western Samoa	Western Samoan(s)	Western Samoan
West Germany	West German(s)	West German

Country or region	Noun (plural ending in parens)	Adjective
Yemen, North (Yemen Arab Republic)	Yemeni(s)	Yemeni
Yemen, South (People's Democratic Republic of Yemen)	Yemeni(s)	Yemeni
Yugoslavia	Yugoslav(s)	Yugoslav
Zaire (formerly Congo-Kinshasa) (no umlaut over *i*)	Zairian(s)	Zairian
Zambia (formerly Northern Rhodesia)	Zambian(s)	Zambian
Zanzibar (now a part of Tanzania)	Zanzibari(s)	Zanzibar
Zimbabwe	Zimbabwean(s)	Zimbabwean

9.3   Names of nations should always be spelled out if possible. On maps and in charts and boxes it sometimes is necessary to abbreviate. Abbreviations for use in such need are listed in 3.8.

NOTES

CHURCH AND CLERGY

Denominations

10.0   Following are names of some representative denominations from the list of more than 200 published by the National Council of the Churches of Christ in the U.S.A.:

African Methodist Episcopal Church

African Methodist Episcopal Zion Church

Assemblies of God

Baptist groups, see below

Christian Church (Disciples of Christ)

Christian Churches and Churches of Christ

Church of Christ, Scientist, see below

Church of Jesus Christ of Latter-day Saints (Mormons), see below

Episcopal Church, see below

Friends groups, see below

Greek Orthodox Archdiocese of North and South America

Hungarian Reform Church in America

Jehovah's Witnesses

Jewish congregations, see below

Lutheran groups, see below

Moravian Church in America

Orthodox Church in America (formerly Russian Orthodox Greek Catholic Church of America)

Pentecostal Assemblies of the World, Inc.

Pentecostal Holiness Church, Inc.

Polish National Catholic Church of America

Presbyterians, see below

Reorganized Church of Jesus Christ of Latter Day Saints

Roman Catholic Church, see below

Romanian Orthodox Episcopate of America

Serbian Eastern Orthodox Church for the U.S. and Canada

Seventh-day Adventists

Syrian Orthodox Church of Antioch

Ukrainian Orthodox Church in America

Unitarian Universalist Association

United Church of Christ (includes the former Evangelical and Reformed Church and most former Congregational Christian churches. Structure and terminology vary; check locally)

United Methodist Church, see below

World Community of Islam in the West (Muslims), see below

Help With Questions

10.1   A valuable aid with names of denominations, church statistics and histories, headquarters addresses and telephone numbers is the *Yearbook of American and Canadian Churches,* published by the National Council of the Churches of Christ in the U.S.A., 475 Riverside Drive, New York, N.Y. 10027. Telephone number of the *Yearbook*: (212) 870-2565. Telephone number of the council's public-relations office: (212) 870-2254. The *Catholic Almanac* is an excellent source on the Roman Catholic Church, but observe our forms as far as they go.

Preferred Forms

10.2   In many denominations a minister is referred to by the honorific *Reverend.* In print this is usually abbreviated to *Rev.,* as follows: the Rev. John J. Pelzer; in subsequent reference Pelzer, or, for a Roman Catholic or for an Episcopal clergyman who prefers it, Father Pelzer. *The Rev. Mr. Pelzer* may be used to distinguish from another Pelzer. Do not write *the Rev. Pelzer, Rev. Pelzer.* The prefatory *the* is necessary in running copy but may be dropped for space reasons in headlines, captions or tabular matter: Rev. John J. Pelzer.

10.3   Sacraments and ceremonies should be cap or lc as indicated in this section.

Sacraments of the Roman Catholic Church, some of which are shared by other denominations—

anointing of the sick, essentially the rite formerly called extreme unction. Say "administered last rites" if that is what they were, or "administered the sacrament" to the person

baptism

confirmation

Eucharist, eucharistic; Holy Communion, Communion, also in some denominations the Lord's Supper

holy orders (ordination ceremonies of the priesthood)

matrimony (the marriage ceremony)

penance

Mass, High Mass, Low Mass, ceremonies at which Communion is administered, are capped when referring to them as abstract rites; lc in mentioning a celebration of the rites—

The central ceremony is the Mass.

The priest said mass in the old church.

Mass is celebrated, read or said. High mass is sung, not held. Low mass is recited, said or read, not sung.

10.4   Sections that follow give correct forms for referring to people and institutions in some of the churches most often in the news. Other denominations have their own titles and structures, which should be checked either locally or at national headquarters as necessary.

10.5   **Baptists** are divided into a number of groups. Two of the major groups are:

American Baptist Churches in the United States, otherwise known as the American Baptists; a member is an American Baptist.

Southern Baptist Convention, known as the Southern Baptists; a member is a Southern Baptist.

The major black Baptist bodies are:

National Baptist Convention of the United States of America, Inc.

Progressive National Baptist Convention, Inc.

National Baptist Convention of America

Other Baptist groups include:

Baptist General Conference (Swedish background)

North American Baptist Conference (German background)

American Baptist Association

Refer to Baptist groups by name; it is incorrect to write "the Baptist church" except in reference to a local congregation.

Baptist groups do not have bishops, but they have a structure of boards and agencies at various levels.

Use of the term "Reverend" is problematic among Baptists. It is best to avoid titles.

Although deacons are ordained to assist pastors and do similar work, they are lay persons, not members of the clergy.

The organizational structure of the groups is somewhat different, but their terminology is similar:

> Southern Baptist Convention; the convention; the denomination
>
> First Baptist Church; the church
>
> John J. Pomeroy, pastor of the First Baptist Church; the pastor; Pomeroy; or John J. Pomeroy, a Baptist minister or clergyman
>
> John J. Pomeroy, a deacon in the First Baptist Church; the deacon; Pomeroy
>
> John J. Pomeroy, executive secretary of the American Baptist Churches in the U.S.A.; the executive secretary; Pomeroy

10.6 **Church of Christ, Scientist** (Christian Scientists); on subsequent reference, the church.

Capstone of the denomination is the Mother Church, named the First Church of Christ, Scientist, in Boston. The Mother Church is run by a five-member board of directors, styled in this fashion:

> Michael (or Jane) Anderson, member of the board of directors; Anderson

Local congregations are called branch churches. Their connection is directly with the Mother Church. They operate according to the church manual of the Mother Church, as does the Mother Church itself.

Branch churches never use *the* before their names. That is reserved for the Mother Church. A local church would be:

> First (or Second, Third, etc.) Church of Christ, Scientist; the church

Any office of the church may be held by either a male or a female.

Clerical titles are not used by the Christian Scientists. A

local congregation may have a first reader and a second reader:

> Mary Johnson, first reader in Second Church of Christ, Scientist; Johnson

> Samuel Jay, second reader in First Church of Christ, Scientist; Jay

Christian Science practitioners work independently of the local churches:

> John (or Elizabeth) Barton, a Christian Science practitioner; Barton

Lecturers are members of the Board of Lectureship of the Mother Church:

> Henry (or Mavis) LaPorte, a Christian Science lecturer

10.7   **Church of Jesus Christ of Latter-day Saints** may be referred to as the Mormon Church in first and subsequent mention if the full name appears at least once in the article. Members may be referred to as Mormons or Latter-day Saints.

There are two divisions of the priesthood: the Aaronic and the Melchizedek. The offices of the Aaronic priesthood, beginning with the lowest: deacon, teacher, priest and bishop. The offices in the Melchizedek priesthood are: elder, seventy, high priest, patriarch and apostle. A person of any ranking from elder up may be referred to as elder: President Walter Beitz of the Riverdale Stake; Elder Beitz.

Organization and terminology:

> President John Smith of the Homeville Branch (a small congregation); President Smith, Elder Smith or Smith; the president (*president* here is equivalent to *pastor*).

> Bishop John Smith of the Centerton Ward (a large congregation); Bishop Smith, Elder Smith or Smith; the bishop (equivalent to *pastor*).

> President John Smith of Upper City Virginia Stake (a group of congregations); President Smith; Elder Smith or Smith; the president

> President John Smith of the Church of Jesus Christ of Latter-day Saints or President John Smith of the Mormon Church; President Smith; Elder Smith; Smith

At Mormon Church headquarters the presiding officer is the first president. The first president and two counselors form the First Presidency; under the First Presidency is the Quorum of Twelve Apostles; under the Twelve is the First Quorum of Seventy. Any member of these groups may be referred to as elder:

> Elder John Smith, an apostle and member of the Quorum of Twelve; Elder Smith; Smith.

An additional body is the Presiding Bishopric, composed of the presiding bishop and two counselors and reporting directly to the first president. The bishopric has responsibility for temporal affairs. Its members are addressed as Bishop:

> Bishop Allison Young; Bishop Young; the bishop; Young

10.8 **Reorganized Church of Jesus Christ of Latter Day Saints** (note *Latter Day*) uses the same terminology for its officials as does its sister church, but calls its divisions by slightly different names. Individual churches are missions, branches and congregations. Missions and branches are responsible to district presidents; district presidents report to regional presidents, and regional presidents to the Quorum of the Council of the 12 Apostles. Congregations, which usually are larger groups and often urban, are organized into stakes, which are responsible to the Apostles.

10.9 **Episcopal Church,** on subsequent reference, is *the church.* Other forms:

> an Episcopalian
>
> Episcopal, adj., not Episcopalian: the Episcopal ritual
>
> the Rev. Andrew (or Janice) Tucker, deacon of St. Dunstan's Episcopal Church; the deacon; Tucker
>
> the Rev. Andrew (or Janice) Tucker, rector of All Souls' Episcopal Church; Tucker (Father Tucker if he prefers); the minister; a minister
>
> Suffragan Bishop Andrew Tucker of Virginia, or of the Diocese of Virginia; Bishop Tucker; Tucker; the bishop

(*the Rt. Rev.* is no longer required for Episcopal bishops, but it is not incorrect and it is the polite form of address to use in a letter.)

> Canon Andrew Tucker; Canon Tucker; the canon; Tucker (usually an ordained person, member of the staff of a bishop or cathedral)
>
> Presiding Bishop Andrew Tucker of the Episcopal Church; Presiding Bishop Tucker or Bishop Tucker; Tucker; the presiding bishop or the bishop

the Very Rev. Andrew Tucker, dean of Birmingham Cathedral; Dean Tucker; Tucker; the dean

10.10   **Jewish congregations** belong to three separate groups:

> Union of American Hebrew Congregations (a reform group)
>
> United Synagogue of America (a conservative group)
>
> Union of Orthodox Jewish Congregations of America (an orthodox group)

Houses of worship are called temples or synagogues:

> Reform congregations, usually temple, as: Temple Beth El; the temple (but check the individual name)
>
> Conservative congregations, usually synagogue, as: Beth Sholom Synagogue; the synagogue (but check the individual name)
>
> Orthodox congregations, always synagogue, as: Agudas Achim Synagogue; the synagogue
>
> Rabbi Samuel Silver; Rabbi Silver; the rabbi
>
> Cantor Ralph Orloff; Cantor Orloff; the cantor

Rabbinical groups:

> Central Conference of American Rabbis (a reform group)
>
> Rabbinical Assembly (a conservative group)
>
> Rabbinical Council of America (an orthodox group)
>
> Union of Orthodox Rabbis (an orthodox group)

10.11   **Lutherans** are organized in three major groups. These groups work together through a common council, the Lutheran Council of the U.S.A., but the council has no governing power. The groups are:

> Lutheran Church in America
>
> Lutheran Church—Missouri Synod
>
> American Lutheran Church

Form for referring to Lutheran pastors of all groups:

> the Rev. Henry Stromberg, pastor of First Lutheran Church; Stromberg

The Lutheran Church in America is divided geographically into synods, headed by synod presidents.

The Lutheran Church—Missouri Synod is divided into districts, headed by district presidents.

The American Lutheran Church is divided into districts, which are headed by district presidents.

10.12 **World Community of Islam in the West** (formerly Nation of Islam, also formerly often called "Black Muslims," properly referred to as Muslims) is open to persons of all races. On subsequent reference, officially WCIW: may also be Islam or the Muslims.

Head of the World Community of Islam in the West is the chief minister. Form:

> Chief Minister Wallace D. Muhammad; Chief Minister Muhammad; the chief minister

Seat of the Community of Islam is Elijah Muhammad's Mosque No. 2 of the Holy Temple of Islam, in Chicago.

Local churches stand in direct connection with the chief minister. They are called mosques. Official names, for example, are Mosque No. 4, Mosque No. 176, etc. The mosques are numbered in national sequence and no two have the same number.

The leader of a mosque is called a minister:

> Minister Nathaniel Muhammad of the Kansas City Mosque; Minister Muhammad

The Community's bible is the Holy Koran.

The newspaper is the *Bilalian News*.

10.13 **Presbyterians** are divided into two main groups:

> Presbyterian Church in the U.S. (the Southern organization)
>
> United Presbyterian Church in the U.S.A. (the Northern organization)

In some places, such as the Washington, D.C., area, the two groups form united presbyteries. The Northern and Southern groups have essentially the same structure and terminology:

> First Presbyterian Church; the church
>
> The Rev. Richard Rouse, pastor, First Presbyterian Church; the pastor; Rouse

Elders are lay persons elected to the post:

> John Doe, an elder of the United Presbyterian Church
>
> Richard Roe, a ruling elder

The stated clerk, an elected official, is the highest executive in the overall church organization. He may be either a lay
person or an ordained minister:

> Richard Roe, stated clerk of the Presbyterian Church in
> the U.S. or:
>
> the Rev. Richard Rouse, stated clerk of, etc.

The general assembly, elected each year, is the top policy-
making body. Members are called commissioners. The head of
the assembly is the moderator, also elected each year.

> Mary Jones, a commissioner to the general assembly;
> Jones
>
> the Rev. Richard Rouse, a commissioner to the general
> assembly; Rouse
>
> Geneva Roberts, moderator of the general assembly
>
> or: the Rev. Dana Perkins, moderator of the general
> assembly

Geographically, the structure is as follows:

> Synods are groups of presbyteries. The Piedmont Syn-
> od, for instance, covers a large territory that includes
> the Washington, D.C., area among others. The head of a
> synod is called the *synod executive*.
>
> Presbyteries are groups of congregations. The National
> Capital Union Presbytery covers the Washington area.
> The head of a presbytery is the *presbytery executive*.

10.14   **Religious Society of Friends:** Shorten to the Society of Friends
on subsequent mention, or to Friends in such subsequent
references as "the Friends' attitude toward war." The Friends
also may be called Quakers.

> The Society of Friends operates through five main groups:
>
> Friends General Conference
>
> Friends United Meeting
>
> Evangelical Friends Alliance
>
> Religious Society of Friends (Conservative)
>
> Religious Society of Friends (Unaffiliated Meetings)

There are also some smaller unaffiliated groups.

A local congregation is a *monthly meeting*, capitalized when part of a name. Some monthly meetings have no clergymen; others have leaders called pastors or executive secretaries:

> John P. Jones, pastor of Oak Grove Friends Meeting

Monthly meetings are organized into *quarterly* or *half-yearly* meetings, and these are grouped into *yearly meetings*, which correspond to dioceses in some other denominations. These terms are capitalized when used in names. Quarterly or half-yearly meetings and yearly meetings are run by officials with the title of clerk:

> Frank Brown, clerk of the Center City Yearly Meeting; Brown

The Society of Friends maintains contacts with the meetings (congregations) of the major organizations through the Friends World Committee for Consultation, to which they send delegates or observers.

10.15   **Roman Catholic Church,** on subsequent reference, is *the church.*

> St. James's Roman Catholic Church; the church; a Roman Catholic church
>
> a Roman Catholic
>
> the Rev. Xavier O'Donnell, pastor of St. James's Roman Catholic Church; the pastor; Father O'Donnell; the priest; O'Donnell

(*priest* is a proper vocational description for ordained persons from a pastor to and including the Pope.)

> Auxiliary Bishop Xavier O'Donnell of Birmingham; Bishop O'Donnell; the bishop; O'Donnell
>
> Bishop Xavier O'Donnell of Atlanta; Bishop O'Donnell; the bishop; O'Donnell

(*the Most Rev.* is no longer necessary for Roman Catholic bishops and archbishops, but it is not incorrect, and in a letter it is the polite form of address. Also, see below.)

> Archbishop Xavier O'Donnell of Richmond; Archbishop O'Donnell; the archbishop; O'Donnell
>
> Cardinal Xavier O'Donnell; Cardinal O'Donnell; the cardinal; O'Donnell

("Xavier Cardinal O'Donnell" is no longer necessary.)

Pope Aloysius XXIII; Pope Aloysius; the Pope; a Pope

Msgr. Xavier O'Donnell; Monsignor O'Donnell; the monsignor; O'Donnell

(*Monsignor* is an honorary title conferred by the Pope on some priests who are not bishops. Do not write, "the Rev. Msgr. Xavier O'Donnell"; one title is enough.)

NOTE: *the Very Rev.* and *the Most Rev.* are used in referring to the superiors general of some Roman Catholic orders.

10.16   **United Methodist Church,** on subsequent reference, is *the church.*

Some nonordained persons serve in special capacities as deacons and deaconesses. They may be described as such but are not officially referred to by a title or an honorific like *the Rev.*

When a lay person supplies a church (serves it as pastor) it is a customary courtesy to put *the Rev.* before his or her name.

Ordained persons first become deacons and then elders. All ordained persons are referred to as *the Rev.* Either a deacon or an elder may be a pastor; to hold a position higher than pastor, one must be an elder.

All titles are used for men and women alike. Women as well as men can be deacons, pastors or bishops.

Terminology:

Tenth Street Methodist Church; the church

the Rev. Harwood Johnson, pastor of Tenth Methodist Church; the pastor; Johnson (may be either a deacon or an elder)

the Rev. Harwood Johnson, district superintendent; Johnson

Bishop Harwood Johnson of the Kentucky Area; Bishop Johnson; the bishop; Johnson

NOTES

WEAPONS, PLANES, ASTRONAUTICS

11.0   Typical items are listed here to show the forms used. For greater detail, *Jane's Weapon Systems* and *Jane's All the World's Aircraft* are helpful. Note some cases in which our style varies from *Jane's*.

Guns

11.1   In the examples that follow, there is no intent to dictate descriptive terms. For instance, the 7.3-mm weapon does not have to be called a pistol. If it is an automatic, it may be so designated.

> 12-gauge shotgun
>
> .410-bore shotgun (the .410 is actually caliber)
>
> .22-caliber rifle
>
> .30-30 rifle (.30 caliber, 30 grains of powder in cartridge)
>
> M-16 rifle
>
> .45-caliber automatic
>
> .32-caliber revolver
>
> 7.3-mm pistol
>
> M-60 machine gun
>
> 75-mm gun
>
> 3-inch, 50-caliber gun

Planes

11.2   **U.S.-made commercial planes** usually are identified by numbers or by combinations of letters and numbers. Some planes also are given appellations, which may be used or omitted as desired. The maker's name also may be used or omitted.

> Lockheed L-1011 TriStar, or L-1011, or Lockheed L-1011, or TriStar
>
> Boeing 707, 727, 737, 747
>
> McDonnell Douglas DC-8, DC-9, DC-10

11.3   **U.S. military planes** customarily are designated by numbers, with prefixed letters to indicate basic functions: A for attack, B for bomber, C for cargo, F for fighter, S for antisubmarine, T for trainer, etc. Often a letter is added at the end to show order in a series, or an adaptation. Appellations, when they exist, may be used or omitted as desired. Examples:

F-4D Phantom or F-4D or Phantom

| B-52H Stratofortress | C-9B | A-4 Skyhawk |
| F-15A Eagle | S-3A Viking | TA-4J Skyhawk trainer |

11.4   **Russian planes** generally are designated by numbers, with prefixes that are abbreviations of the makers' or designers' names: Tu for Tupolev, MiG for Mikoyan & Gurevich, M for Myasishchev, Su for Sukhoi, Yak for Yakovlev, Il for Ilyushin, and others. NATO specialists give appellations to Russian planes, and these names may be used or omitted as desired. Examples:

| Il-76 Candid | Yak-28 Brewer, Firebar and Maestro | M-4 Bison |
| Tu-144 Charger | Su-19 Fencer | MiG-25 Foxbat |

The controversial Backfire bomber had not been given any designation, as of May, 1977, except V-G (variable geometry, because of its movable wings).

11.5   ## Tanks

U.S.	Russian
M47	T-62
M48	T-70
M60	PT-76

Rockets

11.6   Forms for major long-range rockets, space boosters and some others are shown in the examples that follow. Details of the hundreds of specialized battlefield, surface-to-air, air-to-air, air-to-surface and other specialized rockets must be obtained from *Jane's* or military sources. Regardless of *Jane's*, for simplicity all numbers should be in Arabic.

11.7   **U.S. rockets** and rocket stages generally are known by popular names, which sometimes are followed by numerals that stand for model numbers. Examples:

Titan 3	Saturn 5	Minuteman 3
Titan 3D	S-4B (rocket stage)	

Submarine-launched rockets are known by their appellations, sometimes followed by letters and numbers:

Polaris A-2	Poseidon C-3
Polaris A-3	Trident 1

11.8   **Russian strategic rockets** are SS-4, SS-9, SS-14, etc. Russian submarine-launched rockets are SSN-4, SSN-5, SSN-6, SSN-7, SSN-8. Surface-to-air (antiaircraft) missiles are designated by SA and number: for instance, SA-3. Most of these missiles have been endowed with names, but they are usually known by letter and number.

Space Probes and Satellites

11.9   **U.S. satellites** and space-vehicle types usually are referred to by names, with numerals or letters:

Intelsat 4	Agena D

11.10   **Individual U.S. space vehicles and missions** use names, frequently with numerals added to show number in series:

Viking 2	Pioneer 11
GEOS 3 (for Geodynamics Satellite)	

11.11   **Russian space vehicles** and missions are treated generally in the same way:

Cosmos 629	Sputnik 1; a sputnik

11.12   **Space command ships, landers,** moon cruisers, etc. are referred to by name or description without quotes or italics:

Casper (orbiting command ship)	Orion (lander)
Kitty Hawk (command ship)	Antares (lander)
space buggy moon rover	Lunokhod 1
space shuttle (descriptive, not a name)	

NOTES

MEDICAL TERMS

12.0   Medical articles in the press undergo constant criticism and therefore require special care. Of course the first consideration is for the facts; but accepted form, too, indicates authenticity. In form as well as content the primary safeguard is meticulous checking with expert sources, including informed persons and a good medical dictionary. Only a whole book could cover the subject, but it is possible to lay down some principles and cautions.

12.1   **Diseases, conditions and symptoms** generally are printed in roman type and are lower-cased except for proper names they may contain:

measles	Parkinson's disease	neuralgia
osteoarthritis	hyperglycemia	aneurysm
emphysema	Ménière's syndrome	Hodgkin's disease
atherosclerosis	infarction	Peyer's patch or Peyer patch

12.2   **Tests and treatments** also are generally in roman type and are lower-cased except for words that would be capitalized when alone:

tuberculin test	barium X-ray	cobalt therapy
acupuncture	Heimlich maneuver	metabolism test

12.3   **Infectious organisms** are most often referred to by genus and species, as: *Staphylococcus aureus*. The genus is capitalized, the species is lower-cased. Both words are italicized. Once the genus has been named, it may be abbreviated in subsequent mention: *S. aureus*.

Each such organism comes at the end of a long chain of classification. In the traditional system, micro-organisms are divided into phyla, which are divided into classes, then orders, then families, genera and species. Classifications wider than genus will occur infrequently in news copy. When they do, they are capitalized but not italicized. The phylum Nematoda, for instance, is the overall group that includes in its chain the species *Trichinella spiralis*, cause of trichinosis.

Common names exist for some of these organisms, but not for others. The organisms of *T. spiralis*, for example, may be referred to as trichinae, and Nematoda are nematodes.

A *strain* is a variant that may be observed when the same species is isolated from different sources. If specimens of *Streptococcus pyogenes* taken from Doe and Roe show characteristics that are not the same, one may be called the Doe strain and the other the Roe strain.

It takes a comprehensive medical dictionary to verify all the micro-organisms that might appear in copy, but here are a few types to illustrate the forms. One reason for spelling out the genus on first appearance will be seen in the frequency with which the same initial stands for different genera:

Organism	Abbreviation
Bacillus anthracis (causes anthrax)	*B. anthracis*
Babesia bovis (infects cattle)	*B. bovis*
Escherichia coli (intestinal bacterium)	*E. coli*
Salmonella typhi (causes typhoid fever)	*S. typhi*
Salmonella choleraesuis (one of group causing food poisoning)	*S. choleraesuis*
Streptococcus pyogenes (causes "strep throat")	*S. pyogenes*
Staphylococcus aureus (causes boils)	*S. aureus*
Brucella abortus (aborts cows, gives people undulant fever)	*Br. abortus*

To complicate matters, some bacteriologists use descriptive terms such as meningococcus, pneumococcus and typhoid bacillus, which are not part of the classification system. These ordinarily are not capitalized or italicized. They are usable words, and it is not necessary to change them. They can be checked in a medical dictionary or sometimes in the general dictionaries.

12.4   RECOMMENDED: *Stedman's Medical Dictionary*, which is kept on the *USN&WR* Name Checker's desk, and *Dorland's Illustrated Medical Dictionary*.

12.5   **Drugs.** In most cases drugs should be referred to by their generic names rather than by brand names: sulfisoxazole, not Gantricin; tetracycline hydrochloride, not Achromycin.

But if a point is being made about a particular brand, the brand name should be used. In some contexts it may be desirable to use both names, as: "Gantricin, a brand of sulfisoxazole."

Brands generally are capitalized, generic names lower-cased.

For checking, it is desirable to have a book that cross-references brands and generic names.

12.6   RECOMMENDED: *Physicians' Desk Reference* (this is a manual of drugs). A copy is kept on the *USN&WR* Name Checker's desk.

NOTES

TRADEMARKS

13.0 A trademark is a word or symbol used by a manufacturing firm or a business to identify its goods or services. A trademark is legally protected from use by the owner's competitors. It is spelled with an initial capital and usually is employed as an adjective to modify the generic term for the product or service: for example, Argo starch. A trademark must not be lower-cased or used in such a way that it seems to be a common noun or common adjective.

13.1 *USN&WR* policy calls for the use of a generic term rather than a trademark unless a point is being made about a particular trademarked article. Thus for identity's sake we might write about a strike at a plant where Coca-Cola is bottled, but we would not refer to "a labor dispute over operation of the Coca-Cola machine" because *Coca-Cola* is not necessary to this reference; we could say "soft-drink machine."

13.2 If trademarks are not guarded from use in senses that seem generic, they may officially lose protection of the law and can be employed thereafter by all companies. When this happens, there is no longer any restriction on writers. Here is a list of former trademarks that have thus passed into the public domain:

aspirin	kerosene	raisin bran
cellophane	kiddicar	shredded wheat
corn flakes	lanolin	thermos
cube steak	linoleum	trampoline
dry ice	milk of magnesia	yo-yo
escalator	mimeograph	zipper
	nylon	

13.3 Two special cases:

> *jeep*, lower case, is generic for small military vehicles, but when capitalized is a trademark for certain products of American Motors Corporation; for example, Jeep Wagoneer.

> *Deepfreeze* is the trademark of a brand of food freezer, but this cannot govern ordinary use of words by a periodical, as in "Parts of Greenland have been in a deep freeze for years."

13.4 Sources of information about trademarks, including new marks and others not listed in this chapter:

1. *Standard Directory of Advertisers*

2. Style sheets of the United States Trademark Association

3. For drugs, *Physicians' Desk Reference*

4. For telephone inquiries, headquarters of the United States Trademark Association, New York City (212/986-5880)

13.5 Some of the trademarks most likely to be encountered:

A.1 sauce

Acele acetate yarn

Acrilan acrylic fiber

Adrenalin stimulant (BUT: *adrenaline*, a generic term)

Airfoam sponge and cellular rubber

Air-Shuttle (a service of Eastern Air Lines)

Airwick deodorizer

Anchor Fence chain-link fence

Antron nylon yarn

Argo cornstarch and edible oil *

Arnel triacetate

Aureomycin antibiotic

Avlin polyester

Avril rayon

Baggies plastic bags

Band-Aid adhesive bandages *

Boilfast thread

Brillo soap pads

Brown-in-Bag plastic-film bags

Bud beer

Calrod heating units

Celanese acetate/nylon/polyester/rayon/triacetate

Chex cereal

Chiclets chewing gum

Chiffon margarine

Chiffon paper products

Chloromycetin antibiotic

Chromspun acetate fiber

Clorox bleach

Coca-Cola, Coke beverage

Cocomalt beverage mix

Comptometer calculating machines *

Congoleum floor dressings

Cream of Wheat cereal

Crisco shortening

Curity diapers *

Cyclone chain-link fence *

Dacron polyester fiber

Deepfreeze food freezer

Dictaphone dictating machine

Disposall food-waste disposers

Ditto duplicators, copiers, supplies therefor *

Dramamine travel-sickness medicine

Dynel modacrylic fabric

* or other goods sold under that brand

Egg Beaters egg substitute

Electrolux vacuum cleaners *

Energine cleaning fluid *

Estron acetate

Ethyl antiknock compound

Eveready batteries *

Fabrikoid coated fabrics

Fiberglas glass fibers

Fig Newtons cakes

Flit insecticides *

Formica laminated plastic

Fortrel polyester yarns

Frigidaire appliances *

Fritos corn chips

Fudgsicle ice cream on a stick

Gatorade thirst quencher

Gripper snap fasteners

Hamburger Helper packaged
dinner mixes

Hawaiian Punch fruit beverage

Hotpoint appliances *

Hydra-Matic automatic
transmissions

Jeep vehicles (but see above)

Jell-O gelatin dessert *

Jockey brand underwear *

Jonny Mop toilet-bowl cleaner

Kitchen-Tested flour

Kleenex tissues

Kodachrome film

Kodacolor film

Kodak film and cameras *

Kodel polyester

Kool-Aid soft-drink mix

Kotex sanitary napkins, belts,
tampons *

Lastex elastic yarns

Laundromat laundry services
and equipment

Levi's jeans and sportswear

Liederkranz cheese

Linotype typesetting machine *

Lucite acrylic resin

Lycra spandex fiber

Lysol disinfectant

Mace liquid tear-gas
formulation

Masonite hardboard products *

Maypo cereal

Mazola margarine and corn oil

Mercurochrome antiseptic

Miltown tranquilizer

Minute rice *

Mixmaster food mixer

Multigraph duplicating
machine

Multilith offset press

Muzak music programs

Naugahyde vinyl-coated
fabrics *

Neolite composition soles and
heels

Nescafé instant coffee

Nomex nylon

Novocain anesthetic
(BUT: novocaine, generic)

Nutrament food supplement

Oakite household cleaner

Orange Crush beverage

Orinase antidiabetes medicine

Orlon acrylic fiber

Ouija "talking board" sets

Oysterettes crackers

Pablum baby cereal (generic, *pabulum*)

Parcheesi backgammon game

Pepsi beverages

Pepsi-Cola beverages

Philadelphia cream cheese

Photact reproduction materials *

Photostat photographic copy

Ping-Pong table-tennis equipment

Playtex girdles *

Plexiglas acrylic plastic

Pliobond adhesive cement

Pliofilm moistureproof film

Pliolite resin for paints, lacquers

Polaroid photographic equipment *

Polaroid polarizing sunglasses

Polyglas tires

Popsicle frozen confection *

Post Toasties cereal

Postum cereal beverage

Prestone antifreeze *

Pyrex heat-resistant glassware

Q-Tips cotton swabs and cotton balls

Raybestos brake lining

Realtor (property of a trade association; use *real-estate broker, real-estate expert,* etc.)

Ripple ribbed shoe soles

Ritz crackers

Sanforized compressively shrunk fabric

Scotch brand cellophane tape

Scrabble word games

Sen Sen confections

Seven-Up or **7-Up** beverage

Sheetrock gypsum wallboard *

Singer sewing machines *

Soilax cleaner

Spansule sustained-release medication

Styrofoam plastic foam

Suburbanite tires

Sucaryl sweetener *

Sunbeam appliances *

Sunkist fruit and juices

Tabasco sauce

Tabloid drugs and chemicals

Technicolor motion pictures *

Teflon fluorocarbon resins

TelePrompTer cuing apparatus

Teletype teletypewriter and other equipment

Teletypesetter telegraphic typesetting machine

Terramycin antibiotic

Thermo-Fax copying machines

Thiokol liquid polymers *

Thorazine tranquilizer

Tinkertoy construction toy *

Toastmaster electric appliances *

Touch nylon fiber

Touch-Tone pushbutton dialing

Transcendental Meditation

Trevira polyester

TV Dinner frozen dinners

Ultron nylon

* or other goods sold under that brand

Unicap vitamins

Univac computers

Variline thick and thin nylon yarn

Vaseline petroleum jelly, hair tonic *

Verichrome film

Victrola sound apparatus *

Videotape recording tape

Videoscan document reader

Vycron polyester

Webril nonwoven fabric

Xerox electrostatic copiers

Zantrel rayon yarn

Zefkrome acrylic fiber

Zefran acrylic fiber

Zefstat metallic yarn

Zepel fabric fluoridizer

Zerex antifreeze

* or other goods sold under that brand

NOTES

POLITICAL REGIONS OF THE U.S.

(as used by *USN&WR* political analysts)

14.0

EAST (10 states)	*SOUTH* (11 states)	*MIDWEST* (11 states)
New England States Connecticut Maine Massachusetts New Hampshire Rhode Island Vermont *Other States* Delaware New Jersey New York Pennsylvania	Alabama Arkansas Florida Georgia Louisiana Mississippi North Carolina South Carolina Tennessee Texas Virginia	*Big-City States* Illinois Indiana Michigan Ohio *Farm-Belt States* Iowa Kansas Minnesota Nebraska North Dakota South Dakota Wisconsin

(The 10 Eastern states are sometimes referred to as the North Atlantic states; Delaware, New Jersey, New York and Pennsylvania as the Middle Atlantic states.)

Caution: Don't say "North and South Carolina" unless you are prepared for objections. Say "North Carolina and South Carolina" or "the Carolinas."

BORDER (5 states)	*MOUNTAIN* (8 states)	*FAR WEST* (5 states)
Kentucky Maryland Missouri Oklahoma West Virginia	Arizona Colorado Idaho Montana Nevada New Mexico Utah Wyoming	*Pacific States* California Oregon Washington *Other States* Alaska Hawaii

(All five Far Western states are sometimes referred to as the Pacific states.)

NOTE: When an article is based on a source other than *USN&WR*'s own political analysts, follow the regional breakdown used by the source.

NOTES

CAPTIONS, CHARTS, BOXES, CREDITS

Captions

15.0   Captions are and should be written in a variety of forms, but it is useful to sort out the types and to recognize standards for each type.

LABEL CAPTIONS

Topic setters. These usually go under large photos at the start of articles. They are designated by the Art Section for italic type, flush right either over or under the cut. Such a caption should not be a complete sentence and should end in a period:

Bulgarian freighter in the canal.

Names. These usually are caps & lc, centered under cut, no period:

Premier Gondolfo

Composites. The second line ends in a period:

Premier Gondolfo
No place to hide.

Premier Gondolfo
He could not escape.

15.1   **Cartoon captions.** The cartoonist's caption usually is picked up and carried in quotation marks. If the original caption is already a quote—indicating, for instance, words spoken by a character in the cartoon—our caption still uses only one set of quotation marks. Period is used. Cartoon captions usually are centered and clc.

MacNELLY IN *RICHMOND NEWS LEADER*

"A real bad scene."

ACTION CAPTIONS

These are set in roman type (not ital) and generally flush left. Usually they are full sentences, with periods, but they may be less than full sentences, still with periods for uniformity. Examples:

New factory turns out umbrella handles.

Umbrella handles leaving new factory.

Lead-ins and read-ins. Captions for a series of related photos may be started with bold-face words or phrases:

French connection. Mideast cafes get some fancy meat choppers from Paris.

American know-how. U.S. advisers are helping to set up fast-food chains.

Full house is a winner for restaurateur at holiday time; roast goose leads menu.

Early worms get the bird at stadium's ticket window; seats are all sold out.

In a series, this kind of caption should be used throughout or not at all; otherwise appearance is spotty.

15.2   TENSES

Tense of a caption customarily is the present, even if an event long past is pictured. But it is best to avoid absurdities:

AWKWARD: Umbrellas leave the factory last July.

BETTER: Umbrellas leaving the factory last July.

15.3   CONTENT

Care should be used not to embarrass or offend persons in photos. See 1.22.

Charts, Boxes

15.4   Form and treatment of a typical chart or box are shown in the example on next page.

RURAL CROPS: RISING

From 'Simmons to Sorghum, an Increase

For fiscal year 1977—

Commodity	Gain or Loss (in tons)	Percentage of Change
Persimmons	460 mil.	Up 40%
Sorghum	13 mil.	Up 12%

Headings. All caps or clc. In clc headings, cap each word except prepositions *at, by, for, in, of, on* and *to;* the abbreviated preposition *vs.;* conjunctions *and, as, but* and *or;* articles *a, an,* and *the.* Do not cap these words even at the start of a line, except the first. Cap in *Goes On,* etc. See 4.76.

Bank lines under top headings: Rules for caps and lc are same as in headings.

Explanatory copy, either in sentence form with period or nonsentence with dash, colon or dots at end ("For fiscal year 1977—"above): Cap first letter of first word only.

Column headings: Rules for caps and lc are same as in headings.

Stubs—vertical listing of items down left side of chart or box: Cap first letter of first word in each item.

Body—reading across from stubs: Treat same as stubs.

Parenthetical matter—such as "(in tons)" above: all lc except for proper nouns and proper adjectives.

Plotting labels—titles characterizing graph lines or bar charts, etc., usually standing nearby in a strategic place: caps and lc as in headings.

mil. and *bil.,* if these abbreviations are designated by the Art Section: no initial caps.

15.5   **Footnote symbols.** These are used in the order in which they appear in headings, stub and body of a chart or box, and in this sequence:

*

†

**

‡

Notes and footnotes. These end with periods, even when no sentence is formed. Source lines do not.

15.6   STYLE NOTES

Percent is not a noun and should be changed to *percentage* or *proportion* in editing chart and box headings.

Percent mark may be used with figures in charts and boxes.

Dollar amounts may be expressed as $3 million, etc. if Art Section so designates.

Uniformity is desirable in table stubs; similar items should be treated the same, as: printers, mechanics, painters ... NOT: printers, garages, painters. ...

Credits

15.7   Credits are set in capitals. Rules followed for other copy apply as to italicizing and use of quotation marks, accents and abbreviations.

Positions for credits with photos, cartoons and illustrations are indicated by the Art Section on its layouts.

Where photographer and agency are credited together, a dash (rather than a hyphen) is used to link them. This makes the hyphen available for use in a compound name. Examples:

WOLFF—BLACK STAR

HENRI CARTIER-BRESSON—MAGNUM

TOM O'HALLORAN—*USN&WR*

The names of two agencies given credit for the same photo are separated by a slash. Example: GAMMA/LIAISON

When one photographer supplies all the photos for a story, the style is: PHOTOS BY CHRISTOPHER SPRINGMANN

Corporate publicity photos are usually not credited when the company is identified in the caption.

Occasionally a photographer is credited in the story's byline instead of using photo credits.

Note variation in wording for cartoon credits:
OLIPHANT IN *WASHINGTON STAR*
BASSET FOR SCRIPPS-HOWARD

A few cartoonists and photographers require the use of a copyright symbol.

Cartoons should be credited even if a signature is part of the cartoon.

Names of cartoonists, photographers and agencies can be checked with the Art Section or in many cases in the *Editor and Publisher Year Book.*

Source and Basic-Data Lines

15.8   Most charts, maps and boxes have source or basic-data lines.

Source lines are set in capitals and lower case and are usually introduced by *USN&WR*. If more than one source is listed, they are separated by commas unless semicolons are necessary for clarity. Federal agencies are designated as U.S. and—an exception to style followed elsewhere—the abbreviations *Dept.* and *Depts.* are used. Otherwise, the complete name of the agency is given and abbreviations that would not be used in body copy are avoided, as are acronyms, except *USN&WR*, and, occasionally, FBI. Follow general style for italics, quotation marks and accents.

Examples:

> *USN&WR* chart—Basic data: U.S. Depts. of Labor, Commerce; estimates by *USN&WR* Economic Unit
>
> *USN&WR* map
>
> *USN&WR* table—Basic data: U.S. Dept. of the Treasury, *National Geographic*

Avoid complete sentences in source lines and do not use a period at the end.

The Art Section indicates the position of the source line on its layout for the chart or box. Source lines for boxes usually run inside the rules or on the color panel that defines the borders of the box. For charts, the Art Section takes into account the position it has selected for the source line in preparing the page layout and adjusts the column counts accordingly. Sometimes it places source lines outside the apparent boundaries of charts.

The News Desk edits source lines for style and content, and checks their position to make sure that each line covers the portion of the chart to which it applies.

Maps

15.9   Maps take the following styling:

Italic caps and lower case
Gulfs
Rivers
Lakes
Oceans
Channels

Roman caps and lower case
Canals
Cities
Countries

Full caps, roman
Planets
States

Lightface caps or special styling
Counties
Provinces

SLANG, DIALECT, JARGON

16.0   Slang and other nonstandard words create an on-the-scene ambience. They sound best in quotations from others, but we can use them to advantage in our own writing if we do it right. The absolute essential is clarity to all readers. Nonstandard words often are understood only in certain regions or trades or by limited social or ethnic or age-oriented groups. Therefore if we employ such a word we have to make sure, by the context or by a sly explanation, that the meaning is plain.

Do not put quotation marks on nonstandard words unless the intention is to attribute them to individuals or groups identified or implied in the copy. If we have to apologize for a word, we should not write it.

Best guide to use of nonstandard words is a dictionary that not only is up to date but also distinguishes these words by the terms *slang, colloquial, regional* and so on. Webster's New World and the American Heritage Dictionary perform this service thoroughly, and thus they clue us to the treatment needed.

16.1   The list that follows is offered not as a lexicon of slang but only as an illustration of practical usage.

beat, to avoid a penalty (slang). Plenty clear in:

Farnsworth beat that rap, but was sent up for perjury.

beatnik (slang). Clear in nearly all contexts.

bread, for money (slang). Hard to see how we can use this one without attributing and explaining:

He said he held up the bank to get "bread"—his word for money.

bug, to annoy (slang). Usable if we can quote somebody:

Johnson said Boggs was "bugging" him. (Johnson said it.)

bug, to equip with a secret microphone or recording machine (slang). Wide use:

Horwatny complained that his telephone had been bugged by the FBI.

bug off, to stop annoying somebody and leave (slang).

> Johnson invited Boggs to "bug off" and stop bothering him. (Johnson said it.)

bug out, to run away or desert (slang). Hard to see how we can use this one except when quoting somebody.

bull, shoot bull (slang). All right in a relatively informal passage:

> Professor Brown would shoot bull all night with the students. Or: He enjoyed the bull sessions with the undergraduates.

chemistry, defined by American Heritage as "behavior or functioning, as of a complex of emotions." Now in expanded usage, as:

> In his effort to rebuild the company, he had the benefit of good chemistry with the staff.

flaky—screwy, nutty, unconventional, crazy (slang). We would be unwise to apply this to people, as some magazines do. Conceivable in unusual instances, like:

> Follett's play tells the flaky love story of a way-out waitress and an encyclopedia salesman.

fly (intransitive), to operate successfully, to work right. Not in most dictionaries but useful:

> Jones insisted that the scheme would not fly, and in fact it flopped in a few months.

fly right, to behave yourself. Not in most dictionaries, but usable:

> Berwelder was told that he would be fired if he did not straighten up and fly right.

frag, to blow up an unpopular officer or other person, particularly with a fragmentation device (military slang). Best used with quotes the first time attributing the word to persons or groups or locale and time:

> The Vietnam War offense of "fragging"—blowing up unpopular comrades . . .

gut, adj., basic or fundamental, as *gut feelings* or *gut issues.* Good in many contexts:

> Jobs and prices were the gut issues of the 1976 campaign.

gutbucket, adj, designating a raucous style of jazz resembling barrelhouse. It's a standard word. Conceivable for us if we used it in a far-out personality piece:

> They were at Ernie's joint playing gutbucket jazz with the group.

hippie (slang). Clear in nearly all contexts.

joint, a bar, nightclub or other gathering place (slang). In an informal passage:

> He spent some late hours in the joints along Filbert Street.

joint, a marijuana cigarette. Clear in most contexts.

know-how (colloquial). Unlimited use.

plug, to promote (colloquial). Generally clear and usable.

rap, to chat, shoot bull (slang). O.K. in the right context:

> Rapping with the students was a regular activity in his afternoon class.

razz (slang). Good for general use:

> The President was razzed by a crowd at San Diego.

razzmatazz (slang). Generally understandable:

> Filbert ran a noisy campaign, with marching and razzmatazz.

ripoff (now a standard word).

screwy—crazy, nutty, flaky, suspicious (slang). Dangerous to apply to people. Possibly usable in a few cases, such as:

> Just before the car blew up, Lawson sensed something screwy and jumped out.

tap, as a telephone line, by attaching a listening device (standard).

uptight, tense (slang). Pictorial, clear in most connections; two words in predicate:

> The uptight warlords of Angola . . .

> BUT: He was up tight over the examinations.

yak, to chat (slang). Usable if the setting is favorable:

> Yakking over the back fence with neighbors . . .

NOTES

COMPOUND WORDS

How to Form and Style Them

17.0   PROCEDURE:

1. Follow the Word List for words it contains.
2. Then follow the dictionaries as far as they go, with exceptions noted here.
3. Then follow the principles for making up your own combinations.

17.1   **Made-up modifiers.** When you put words together to describe another word, don't make the reader stop and figure out which words go with which; hyphenate. It's all very well for the lexicographers to say the hyphen is disappearing, but where it speeds reading we need it. Look at this example from one of the nation's 10 greatest newspapers:

> hazardous research trailer

How hazardous was the trailer? Not at all; it was a trailer where people carried on hazardous research. So why not say

> hazardous-research trailer

and save a reader's time?

17.2   **Nouns of the moment.** Some combinations have been used so often as nouns that the dictionary recognizes them as single words. But phrases you put together to serve momentary purposes do not thereby become solidified; the dictionary does not find them widely enough used. Examples:

> bookshop, drugstore (sanctified by the dictionary)

> pen shop, doughnut store (not familiar compounds)

Thus, if they're not in the dictionary, don't set them solid.

17.3   **Complex verbs.** Noun combinations used as verbs are solid or hyphened. Check the dictionary. Use the hyphen if you make up your own:

> You should horsewhip that fellow. (dictionary)

He blue-penciled my story mercilessly. (dictionary)

Jones three-putted the nineteenth hole. (made up)

17.4   **Compounds in predicate.** Permanent compounds—those in the dictionary—usually should stay in combination (hyphenated or solid) when occurring as modifiers in the predicate or otherwise after words modified. If a modifier can be considered simply a group of words assembled for a momentary purpose, drop the hyphen.

a well-bred young man	a man too well-bred to complain
an ill-natured child	The child was ill-natured.
a well-prepared student	He came well prepared.

17.5   **-*ly* in multiple modifiers.** When the first word is an adverb, no hyphen is used:

a badly documented argument

When the first word is an adjective, such as *comely, homely, hourly, sprightly,* etc., hyphenate:

hourly-pay issue

sprightly-grandma pose

17.6   **Color combinations.** These are hyphened before nouns they modify, separate in the predicate:

blue-green dress; the dress was blue green

bright-red wagon; the wagon was bright red

17.7   **Prefixes.** Words beginning with the prefixes *ante, anti, bi, co, counter, de, ex, extra, fore, infra, inter, intra, non, out, over, post, pro, semi, trans, ultra, un, under,* etc. are solid combinations—single words—with certain exceptions:

A hyphen is used to promote easy reading–

when a vowel would otherwise be doubled or a consonant tripled: *pre-empt, anti-inflation, bell-like* and so on, but not in *cooperate* or *coordinate;*

when sound or sense would be confused: *co-worker,* not *coworker; co-author,* not *coauthor; non-nuclear,* not *nonnuclear; intra-uterine,* not *intrauterine; pro-union,* not *prounion; co-ed,* not *coed; anti-abortion,* not *antiabortion;*

when a prefix is hung on a capitalized word: *pre-Columbian;*

when a newly formed word resembles one with an established but different meaning:

The plaster cast broke and had to be re-formed.

Work included re-creation of the old tavern.

She re-covered the chair with damask.

Pre-judicial procedures were begun at once.

when a prefix has two standard meanings, one of which is distinguished by use of a hyphen:

exculpate, to free from blame

ex-policeman, a former policeman

(note also Latin phrases such as *ex cathedra*)

extraordinary, out of the ordinary

extra-ordinary, especially ordinary

17.8   For treatment of specific compounds, see the Word List.

NOTES

INDEX AND WORD LIST

(Decimal figures are paragraph numbers; figures at right are page numbers.)

administration, lc except in   41
names: Grant administra-
tion; Federal Energy
Administration, the
administration. 4.0

adviser

after (-)

afterburner
after-dinner (adj)
aftereffect
afterlife
aftershock
aftertaste
after-tax
afterthought

AG. After company name,   18
no comma between, 3.3

age 42 (not aged 42)

agency, cap only in name,   41
4.5

agenda. Acceptable as sing,   8
1.26

Ages. Figures for all, 6.1   83

Agreement. Cap as part of   47
official name; lc stand-
ing alone. 4.27

air (-)

air bag
air base
airborne
airbus
air conditioner
air-condition (v)
air-conditioned (adj)
airdrop (n)
air-drop (v)

airfield
airframe
air gun
air lane
airlift
airline (transporter)
American Airlines
Eastern Air Lines
National Airlines
air line (straight dis-
tance through air)
airliner
airmail
airman
air-minded
air-mobile—but: First
Cavalry Division
(Airmobile)
airport
air power
airspeed
airstrip
airtight
air transport
airway

Air-Shuttle, a trademark
of Eastern Air Lines

Alabama. Abbn *Ala.*

Alabamian

Alaska. No abbn

Alaskan

all (-)

all-American
all-around or all-round
all out (adv) (go all out)
all-out (adj) (all-out
effort)
all right (not alright)

Allah, cap

Alley. Cap in address,   60
4.77

Alliance. Cap as part of   47
official name; lc stand-
ing alone. 4.27

Allied forces, commands   48, 52
and titles, capitalization of,
4.31 and 4.44

Allies, Allied. Cap only as   47
part of well-recognized
name or in reference to
group bearing that name.
See 4.26

a.m.

Ambassador Jarrel Jester;   51
Jarrel Jester, ambassador
to the Always Isles; the
ambassador; an ambassador;
but Ambassador to U.N. 4.43

Amendment. Cap only in name:
Fifth Amendment, the amendment; an amendment

Ampersand (&). Use for *and*   18
in company names, 3.3

Anglicize, cap

anointing of the sick, lc,   122
10.3

Antarctica, cap

Antarctic, the, cap

ante (-), solid except
before *e* or cap or in
classical expressions

antecedent
antechamber
antemeridian
ante meridiem (a.m.)
ante rem, ante res
anterevolutionary

anti (-), solid except before *i* or cap, or in
confusing combinations

anti-abortion
antiaircraft
anti-ballistic-missile
system, ABM (3.17)
anti-bias
antibiotic
anti-American
antichrist
antidote
anti-intellectualism
antimatter
antitrust
anti-union

anti-Semitic, describes
persons who hate or
oppress Jews. Do not
use for Jews or gentiles
who oppose Israeli poli-
cies

any (-)

anybody
anyhow
anyone
anyplace (adv)
(in any place, to any
place, can't go
anyplace)
anytime (or at any time)
any more

atomic power plant

AT&T; but: ITT

Attorney General. Pl attor- 27, 50
neys general. Abbreviate
and cap before full name,
spell out before surname,
3.12; 3.13; cap after name or
alone for federal, lc for
state. 4.43

Aug. When to use, 3.9 25

auto (-)

auto driver
auto maker
automate
auto repairman
auto worker

autobahn, —s (not ital)

Autos. Two-door sedan, 83
V-8, etc., 6.2

Avenue. Spell out and
capitalize when part of
address

a while. O.K. in "a while
ago," "wait a while"

awhile, adv. Means *for a
while,* so it's illogical
to say "for awhile"

ax, axes

B

B-52, B-52s, etc.
11.2-11.4 133

baby-sitter (n)
baby-sit (v)
baby-sitting (n) (adj)

back (-)

backache
backbite (v)
backcountry
backdate
back door (n)
backdoor (adj)
backdown (n)
back down (v)
back fence (n)
back-fence (adj)
backflash
backflow
backlash
backpedal (v)
backrest
back stairs (n)
backstairs (adj)
backstop
backswing
back talk
backtrack (v)
back track (n)
backup (n)
back up (v)
back yard (n)
backyard (adj)

(-) back

cutback (n)
cut back (v)
drawback
call-back (n)
flashback
pullback
rollback

backlash, no quotes

bacteria. Singular is
bacterium; don't write
"a bacteria"

baht, pl bahts. Currency
of Thailand

balboa, pl balboas.
Currency of Panama

bandwagon

baptism (religious), lc, 10.3   123

Baptists, 10.5   123

barnstorming

Baron, when to cap, 4.45   52

Baronet, 4.45   52

baroque

barrel, —s. bbl., use
abbn only in charts,
boxes, maps

Bastille Day

battle (-)

    battle-ax
    battle cruiser
    battle cry
    battlefield
    battlefront
    battleground
    battle-scarred
    battleship

battle-wise

bay. Lc except when part   58
of name: Mobjack Bay,
the bay; BUT Bay Area,
around San Francisco.
4.70

beachhead

bear market (n)
bear-market (adj)

beat (the rap, etc.).   155
Usable when clear, 16.1

beatnik. Usable when clear.

bedrock

belt. Combinations corn
belt, black belt, etc. lc

belt tightening (n)
belt-tightening (adj)

benzene, solvent from coal
gas or tar

benzine, solvent or fuel
from petroleum

Bessemer steel

between: "between 1976 and
1977," not "between 1976
to 1977"

B.C. Follows year; no
comma between

bi (-), combines solid
except before cap or *i*

biannual, twice a year,
semiannual; for every
two years, say biennial

bias, avoiding, 2.0-2.5   13

Bible, the; but: a bible

Bible belt. Can be offensive   13
to many people.
Don't use except when
quoting someone, 2.1

biennial, every two years;
for twice a year, say
biannual or semiannual

big-city states, 14.0   147

Big Four, Big Three, Big Two

big government. Lc like
big business

bil., for billion, —s
(charts, boxes, maps)

bill. Lc for legislation   44
even in name, 4.17

billions, millions, 6.9   85

Bill of Rights

biofeedback

birth (-)

birth control
birthday
birthplace
birth rate (cf. death
rate)
birthright

bishop, use or nonuse,   123
10.5-10.16

biweekly, once every two
weeks; for twice a week,
say semiweekly

black belt

black (-)

blacklist (n,v)
black market (n)
black-market (v, adj)
blackout

blastoff (n)
blast off (v)

bloc. Any group of groups
or group of persons with
a common purpose. Not
necessary to say *block*

blockbuster

bloodbath

bloodstream

blowout

blowup

blueprint

blue ribbon for best yearling bull (lc)

board, cap only in name, 4.5   41

boardinghouse

boat people (no italics)

boatyard

bobby socks (n)
bobby-sox (adj)
bobby-soxer (n)

bohemian. Lc except when it means from Bohemia

bolivar, pl bolivars. Currency of Venezuela

Bomb, the: A- or H-

bombsight

Book titles. Cap or lc as book does, 4.79   61
Italicize, 5.57   77

book (-)

    bookkeeper
    book review
    bookshelf
    bookshop
    book value

(-) book

    bankbook
    checkbook
    notebook
    order book
    pocketbook (wallet or purse)
    reference book
    storybook
    textbook

Border states, 14.0   147

(-) bound

    brassbound
    deskbound
    eastbound
    muscle-bound
    snowbound
    Washington-bound
    westbound
    duty-bound worker is duty-bound to serve
    honor-bound husband is honor-bound to be true
    homeward-bound ship is homeward bound

box (-)

    boxcar
    box office (n)
    box-office (adj)
    box score
    box seat
    box spring
    boxwood

Boxes, 15.4-15.6   150
    Footnotes, 15.5   151

Brackets to enclose matter   80
    inserted into quotes, 5.78

brain (-)

brain trust
brain-truster
brainwash
brainwasher
brainwashing

Brazilian names, 8.18   103

bread, money. Use if attributed and clear.

breadbasket

breadline

break (-)

breakdown
breakthrough
breakup
break-in

bridgehead

briefcase

brightwork

British thermal unit, —s:
B.t.u., spell out first
time

Brothers. Spell out and   18
cap as part of company
name, 3.3

brush (-)

brush fire (n)
brush-fire (adj)
brushoff

Brussels sprouts, 4.82   62

budget, federal, lc

budget message, lc

bug, to annoy. Slang, use   155
if attributed, 16.1

bug, to equip with a hidden   155
listening device. Use
freely, 16.1

bug off, to leave. Use if   156
attributed, 16.1

bug out, to run away. Only   156
in quoting, 16.1

Buildings. Generally capped,   61
4.80
Don't quote names, 5.47   75

bull market (n)

bull-market (adj)

bull, shoot bull. O.K. in
passage

business's (possessive)

buyers' market

C

cabinet, advisory council   41
of a government, lc. 4.3

Cabinet members. Cap titles   50
after names or alone, but
not in generic sense: the
Secretary of State, a

secretary of state. Below
cabinet rank, titles
after names or alone are lc., 4.43

calfskin

California. Abbn *Calif.*

Californian

call (-)

call-back (n)
call-down (n)
call-off (n)
call-out (n)
call-over (n)
call-up (n)

calorie, —s: cal. Use
abbn only in maps,
boxes, charts

Canal Zone. Abbn *C.Z.*

Canada

Abbns of pro-   20
vinces and territories,
3.6.
Residents of
provinces, 9.1   109

cancel, canceled, canceling,
BUT: cancellation

canton. Lc except in name: 58
the canton of Lucerne;
the canton, a canton, cantons.
4.67

Capitalization, 4.0-4.93   41

committees, 4.50-4.51
education, 4.58-4.63
geographic, 4.64-4.72
governmental, 4.0-4.20
headlines, 4.76
international blocs, etc., 4.26-
4.29
military, 4.30-4.39
organizations, functions, 4.52-
4.57
political parties, 4.22-4.25
religion, 4.46-4.49
titles, 4.40-4.45
United Nations, 4.21
miscellaneous, 4.77-4.93

capital gains

capital-gains tax

Captions, 15.0-15.3; 1.22   149

cartoons, 15.1
offense, avoid, 1.22   7
tenses, 15.2

cardinal numbers (and ordinal), spell out nine
and under

carloading (freight)

carry (-)

carryall
carry-back
carry-forward
carryout
carry-over

carte blanche (roman)

Cartoon captions, 15.1   149

case (-)

    casebook
    caseharden
    case history
    case load
    casework
    caseworker

cast-iron ware
    (but: ironware)

catchall

Catholic: If you mean Roman
    Catholic, say it all

CB (adj, n) citizens'-band (radio)

CDT. See Time

cease-fire

Celsius, formerly centi-
    grade, C; degrees
    Celsius, °C

center around. Can't happen,
    but something can center
    on, cluster around, etc.

centimeter: cm, spell out
    first time except in charts, boxes,
    etc.

Central. Cap in name, lc as   58
    descriptive, 4.65

Central American (n, adj)

Centuries, 6.18   88

CFA franc, pl CFA francs.
    Currency of Benin, Cameroon,
    Central African Empire, Gabon,
    Ivory Coast, Niger, Senegal,
    Togo, Upper Volta

Chapter. Cap as in Chapter
    II

Charts, 15.4-15.6   150
    Footnotes, 15.5

check (-)

    checkbook
    checklist
    checkoff
    checkout
    checkpoint
    checkup

chemistry, relations be-
    tween people. Usable
    where clear

Chicano. Acceptable to
    many Mexican Americans,
    but use care about indi-
    viduals

Chief Justice. Cap even
    after name or alone. 4.43   50

Chinese names, 8.12   102

Christmas Eve

Church and Clergy,10.0-10.16 121

anointing of the sick, 10.3
baptism, 10.3
Baptists, 10.5
bishop, 10.5-10.16
Church of Christ,
    Scientist, 10.6
Church of Jesus Christ
    of Latter-day Saints, 10.7
Communion, 10.3
confirmation, 10.3
deacon, 10.5 *ff*
denominations, 10.0
Episcopal Church, 10.9
Eucharist, eucharistic, 10.3
forms, preferred, 10.2-10.16
help with questions, 10.1
Jewish congregations, 10.10
Lutherans, 10.11
Mass, 10.3
Methodists, 10.16
monsignor, 10.15
Most Rev., limited use, 10.15
Nation of Islam, 10.12
officials, 10.4-10.16
pastor, 10.5-10.16
priest, 10.15
Presbyterians, 10.13
Religious Society of
    Friends (Quakers), 10.14
Reorganized Church of
    Jesus Christ of Latter
    Day Saints, 10.8
Roman Catholic Church, 10.15
Rt. Rev., limited use, 10.9
sacraments, 10.3
Synagogue or Temple, 10.10
World Community of
    Islam in The West, 10.12

Church of Christ, Scientist,   124
10.6

Church of Jesus Christ of
Latter-day Saints, 10.7   125

Church of Jesus Christ of   126
Latter Day Saints, Re-
organized, 10.8

Circle. Spell out and cap
in address

citizens'-band radio (CB)

city. New York City; the   43
    city, 4.11

city governments and their
    agencies, 4.11   43

civil rights (n)
civil-rights (adj)
Civil Rights Act

Civil Service. Cap for U.S.   44
    commission and employes
    of commission; lc for
    civil-service system and
    government employes under
    the system. 4.15

clean-up

clear-cut

close-up (n), a picture or
    view from close up

club (-)

club car
clubhouse
clubman
club owner
club sandwich
club soda

co (-). Solid except before   160
    cap or *o* or in confusing
    combinations; co-author,
    co-ed, co-worker. But:
    cooperate, coordinate, 17.7

committee

of Congress: cap in name, 42
lc alone, 4.9
of political party: cap
Democratic National Com-
mittee but lc finance
committee, 4.50, 4.51
private: cap in name of
an organization, as
Committee for Economic
Development; lc for ad
hoc group, such as mem-
bership committee of
the lodge. 4.50, 4.51

Commons, the, British, cap.

communication, act of communi-
cating

communications equipment,
industry, etc.

Communion, Holy
Communion. Cap. 10.3 123

Communism

Communist, etc., when 46
to cap, 4.24

Company. Spell out and cap 54
as part of name, lc alone.
May be abbreviated in
box, chart. Not always
needed if clear. Use &,
not *and.* 3.3, 4.52

company names. How to 18, 54
style them, 3.3, 4.52

Compass directions. Spell 19
out in running copy; ab-
breviate in maps, charts,
boxes, addresses. 3.4

Compound sentences don't 65
always need commas, 5.2

Compound words, 17.0-17.8 159

procedure, 17.0
-ly, 17.5
modifiers, made-up, 17.1
nouns, made-up, 17.2
compounds in predicate, 17.4
prefixes, 17.7
(For individual words,
see lists appearing
alphabetically in this
index)

Conference. Cap as part of 55
full official name, 4.57

confirmation (religious), lc

congressional, lc

congressional district, lc: 58
the third congressional
district. 4.68

congressman. Not a synonym
for member of the House;
Senators also are congressmen. But *congressmen* can
be used for a group of
members of Congress, in
whichever house

Connecticut. Abbn *Conn.*

Connecticuter

conservative, liberal, as 74
political faiths: no
quotes, but caution, 5.42

Constitution. Cap in name   45
or alone when referring
to a national or state
constitution, 4.20

consumer price index

Continent, the. Cap for Europe
only: the Continent. But: the
continent of Europe. Asia, the
continent, lc, and others the
same

continental U.S. Don't use
for the states below
the Canadian border, because
Alaska too is on the con-
tinent. Say *the Lower
48*, or *the Lower 48
states*, or in a real
bind, *the 48 contiguous
states*.

Conventions, political, lc: 46
Democratic national con-
vention, etc. 4.25

co-op. Hyphenate for a
cooperative; otherwise,
it's a home for chickens

cooperation

coordination

cop-out (n)

corn belt

Corporation. Spell out and   54
cap as part of name, lc
alone. Not always needed
if clear. Use **&**, not *and*.
3.3, 4.52

cost-plus-fixed-fee contract

Council. Cap in name, lc   54
alone. But: U.N. Security
Council, the Council. 4.53

councilor, member of a
council. Counselor gives
advice

counselor gives advice.
Councilor is member of
a council

Count, when to cap, 4.45   52

countdown

counter (-): combines solid
except before cap

Countries. Use *it, its*, not
she, her.

Countries, names of. Spell
out where possible, even
on maps
abbreviations in case of
    need, 3.8   20
nationals (citizens), 9.2   110
adjectives of nationality,
    9.2   110

County: Tazewell County; the   43
county. 4.11

County governments and their 43
agencies, 4.11

Courts. Cap names; lc court
in subsequent mention,
except for U.S. Supreme
Court. 4.13   43

cover-up

crack (-)

    crackbrain
    crackdown (n)
    crack down (v)
    crackpot
    crackup

Credits

    cartoon, 15.1   149
    charts, maps, photos,
      15.7   152

criteria. The singular is
criterion; don't write
"a criteria"

cropland

cross (-)

    cross-country
    crosscurrent
    cross-examine
    cross fire (n)
    cross-fire (v)
    crossover
    cross-purpose
    cross-reference
    crossroad
    cross section (n)
    cross-section (v)
    cross-town

cruzeiro, pl cruzeiros.
Currency of Brazil

CST. See **Time**

Cultural designations—ba-   62
roque, existentialism,
etc.—usually lc unless
from proper name. But:
sophist. See 4.83

"cultural revolution" (in
Communist China)

Currencies, foreign

    country by country, 7.0   91
    periodicals about, 7.1   96

cut (-)

    cutback
    cutoff
    cutover
    cutthroat
    cutup

D

da. When surname stands
alone, repeat particle
unless individual drops;
cap or lc as in full
name. 8.6   98

dairy belt

dam. Lc except when part
of a name: Grand Coulee
Dam, the dam. 4.70   58

Darwinian, 4.83   62

Dash, 5.20-5.26   69

    emphasis may be ob-
      tained by, 5.24
    interrupted quote may be
      ended with, but use
      three dots if simply
      trails off, 5.25
    may introduce section or
      entire article, 5.23
    overuse, examples, 5.26
    parenthetical expression
      may be set off by, 5.21
    series may be intro-   69
      duced by, 5.22

data. Plural: "these data,"
    not "this data." If you
    don't like that, say
    "information"

dateline

Day. Cap in name of holiday   62
    or special day, as Elec-
    tion Day, 4.84

de. When surname stands   98
    alone, repeat particle
    unless individual drops.
    Cap or lc as in full
    name. 8.6

    Usually lc in French   102
      names, 8.14

de (-): generally combines   160
    solid except before cap
    or *e*, 17.7

deacon, 10.5-10.16   124

dead (-)

    deadline
    deadlock
    deadwood

death (-)

    deathbed
    death knell
    death rate
    death row
    deathtrap
    death warrant
    deathwatch

Dec. When to use, 3.9   25

Deepfreeze. Trademark of   141
    a brand of food freezer,
    but cannot restrict uses
    such as "the country is
    in a deep freeze," 13.3

de Gaulle. Lc *de* even when   98
    surname stands alone, 8.6

Degrees, academic, 4.60   17, 56

Delaware. Abbn *Del.*

Delawarean

delegate-at-large

Deletions, 5.30-5.34   71

demi (-), solid except be-
    fore *i* or cap

Democratic Party; the party

Denominations, church, 10.0   121

Department. Cap in name of
    primary agency of govern-
    ment; otherwise lc. 4.54;   54
    also, 4.5   41

des
  When surname stands   98
    alone, repeat particle
    unless individual drops;
    cap or lc as in full name, 8.6
  usually cap in French   102
    names when at start of
    surname, 8.14

DES, diethylstilbestrol

Descriptive clauses, set off
  by commas, 5.4   66

(-) **designate**, hyphen as in
  chairman-designate

destroyer escort

détente, no italic

deutsche mark, deutsche
  marks. West German
  currency, commonly
  called the mark, marks

Devil, the; but a devil

Dictionaries
  USN&WR standard, 1.37   10
  names, don't italicize   77
    or quote, 5.57

die (-)

  die-cast (adj)
  die casting (n)
  diehard (n, adj)

dinar, pl dinars. Currency
  of Algeria, Bahrain, Iraq,
  Jordan, Kuwait, Libya,
  Tunisia, Yemen-Aden,
  Yugoslavia

Dirty words. If not using, sub   5
  three asterisks, 1.15

disc. *Disk* is standard except in specialized uses.
  See below and see dic-
  tionary.

disc, phonograph record

disc harrow

disc jockey

Diseases, 12.1   137,138
  reference books, 12.4

disk, standard spelling
  but see special uses as
  disc

disk brake

disk wheel

District of Columbia, the District.
  Abbn *D.C.*

**District of Columbia resi-
  dents**

dive-bomb (v)

dive bomber (n)

Division. Cap in name of   54
  primary agency of gov-
  ernment; otherwise lc.
  4.54

do (particle in name).   98
    When surname stands
    alone, repeat particle
    unless individual drops;
    cap or lc as in full
    name. 8.6

doctor. Remember that den-
    tists are doctors, too,
    so don't say "doctors
    and dentists." "Physicians
    and dentists" is O.K.

Doctrine. Cap in recognized   47
    name; lc alone. 4.28

dollar, —s: dol., dols.,
    use abbn only in maps,
    boxes, charts

dollar-a-year man

dong, pl dong. Currency
    of Vietnam

do's and don'ts. The dic-
    tionary way; illogical
    but the only practical
    solution

double (-)

    double check (n)
    double-check (v)
    double cross (n)
    double-cross (v)
    double-crosser
    double dipping
    double talk

Double modifiers
    simplify, 1.4   2
    made-up combinations
        often need hyphens, 17.1 159

Dow Jones

down (-)

    downgrade
    downhill
    down payment
    downriver
    downside
    downstate
    downswing
    downtrend
    downturn
    down under (Australia
    or New Zealand, but
    down-under policies)

(-) down

    breakdown
    call-down
    clampdown
    countdown
    letdown
    shakedown
    showdown
    slowdown
    step-down
        (all nouns)

Dr. Use for medical doctors   17
    and dentists only, 3.2

drachma, pl drachmas. Cur-
    rency of Greece

(-) driver

    auto driver
    cabdriver
    slave driver
    truckdriver

drop (-)

    drop-in
    drop off (v)
    drop-off (n)
    drop out (v)
    dropout (n)

drought

Drugs.   139
    Use generic name
      unless point is being
      made of brand.
    type treatment, 12.5
    reference book, 12.6

drugstore

drumfire

dry goods (n)
dry-goods store

du, particle in names. When   98
    foreign surname stands alone,
    repeat unless individual
    drops (8.6); in American
    names, cap or lc alone as
    in full name (8.2), except Du
    Pont Company (8.3); usually
    cap in French names, 8.14

due. O.K. when *due* modifies
    a noun: "rain due to a
    cold front," or "autos
    due this fall"; wrong in
    "he went due to urgency."
    Due is an adjective, not
    adverb

Duke, when to cap, 4.45   52

Du Pont. E.I. du Pont de   97
    Nemours & Company; but
    the Du Pont Company, Du
    Pont in references to the
    company. Family branches
    vary spelling. 8.3

dust bowl

Dutch door, 4.82   62

Dutch oven

duty-free goods, these
    goods moved duty-free

dyestuff

E

Earl, when to cap, 4.45   52

earmark (n, v)

earth. Usually lc but see   59
    exceptions at 4.74

earthmover

east, eastern. Direction,   57
    lc; name, cap. 4.64

East Room (of White House)

easygoing

easy-money (adj)

Economic Report (Presi-
    dent's). Capped because
    it is name of a document

Economic Unit (of *USN&WR)*

EDT. See **Time**

Egyptian-Israeli Peace Treaty

-elect (as suffix, hyphen)

Election Day

Electoral College

electronic equipment, etc.
(it's electronic)

electronics industry (concerned with electronics)

Ellipsis, when and how to use, 5.30

Embassies. Cap in name, lc   61
alone, 4.80

employe

en (-)

 enclose
 endorse
 enforce (but *reinforce*)
 enroll

Encyclopedias, don't ital-   77
icize or quote names, 5.57

En dash, may sub for   76
hyphen to avoid confusion, 5.54

engine: airplane engine,
not motor; auto engine
if it's internal-com-
bustion; electric motor

-engine, not engined; four-
engine plane

en route

Episcopal Church, 10.9   126

escudo, pl escudos. Currency
of Portugal

EST, eastern standard time;
abbreviation is customary
as in 5 p.m. EST, but
words may be spelled out
if that is desired.

Establishment, the

Ethnic bias, 2.0-2.4   13

Eucharist, 10.3   123

Eurodollar

even (-)

 evenhanded
 even money
 even-money (adj)
 even-tempered

every day (adv), he goes
every day

everyday (adj), an everyday
trip

ex: separate in Latin
phrases: *ex officio,* 17.7   160

ex (-)   160
from, out; combines
solid as in *expel,* 17.7
former: hyphened as in
ex-policeman, 17.7

Exact words. Say factory, for
example, not facility, 1.6   2

excess-profits tax

excise-tax law

fire (-)

firearm
fireball
firebomb
firebreak
firebrick
fire-eater
firefighter
fire-hardened
firehouse
firepower
fireproof
fire resistance
fire-resistant
fire screen
firestorm
firetrap
fire wall

first-class (adj)

first come, first served
first-come, first-served policy

firsthand information
but: at first hand

first in, first out
first-in, first-out system

flaky, nutty or far out.   156
Unsafe re people. Some
limited use. 16.1

flare-up

flat-footed: a flat-footed
statement; he came out
flat-footed

flatiron

flattop

flat-topped

flier

Florida. Abbn *Fla.*

Floridian

fly, to work right. Usable   156
slang within limits, 16.1

fly right, to behave oneself.
O.K. when clear

f.o.b.

(-) fold: as suffix, solid:
threefold

following. Right: the talk
following the luncheon
(it's an adj). Wrong: He
talked following the
meeting (don't use as adv).

foodstuffs

foot, feet: ft. Use abbn
only in charts, boxes,
maps

foot-and-mouth disease

Footnotes, 15.5   151

footwear

fore (-): combines solid   160
except before cap or *e*,
17.7

forego, to go before;
forgo, to relinquish

French-fried onions

French leave

French names, 8.13, 8.14   102

Friends, Religious Society
  of, 10.14   129

fringes, meaning fringe
  benefits: no quotes

front line (n)
front-line (adj)

front-runner

full (-)

  full-blooded
  full-bodied
  full-fledged
  full-scale
  full-time (adj), but:
    working full time

funky, earthy, etc.: O.K.
  in informal context, but
  careful about people

further: concerned with abstract relationships
  of degree or quantity; also
  means *more* or *additional*,
  as in "further reasons."
  See *farther*

G

gallon, —s: gal., use
  abbn only in charts,
  boxes, maps

Gen. Abbreviate before   28,51
  full name, spell out
  before surname; lc in
  mention without name,
  3.14, 4.43

Gender. Countries are *it*,
  ships are *she*.

Geographic names,   10
  spelling of, 1.38
  abbreviation of, 3.5-3.8   19

Geographic terms, capi-
  talization of, 4.64-4.72   57

Georgia. Abbn *Ga.*

Georgian

German names. If name uses   103
  umlaut, don't substitute
  e, 8.15

German nouns. Capitalize if
  used as foreign words, in
  italic; lc if Anglicized,
  in roman

Gerunds, 5.72   79

ghetto, pl ghettos. Incorrect
  when used for a section
  populated by minority persons,
  unless under legal compulsion

ghostwrite

ghostwriter

GI, **GI's** (lc *s* even in all-cap heads)

GI Bill

giveaway

glamour, glamorous

GM, O.K. for General Motors after spelling out once. In a group of companies or in typewriter features, may be used first time if clear

GmbH. After company name, 18 no comma between, 3.3

go-ahead (n, adj)

God. Cap for Supreme Being; 52 lc for just any old god; cap names of God; cap appellations meaning God; cap names of lesser gods. Cap He, His, Him but not who, whose, whom. 4.46

(-) **goer**: combines solid except when awkward combination would result:

churchgoer
operagoer
theatergoer
Mardi Gras goer
strawberry-festival-goer

going-over

goings-on

goodbye

Good Friday

good will (n)

good-will (adj)

GOP. Acceptable for Republican Party; no periods

Gov. for Governor: Use only in series, charts, boxes, maps

government, lc except in 41 names: the U.S. government; Government Employees Insurance Company, 4.0

Governor April Forman of 51 Idaho; the governor; a governor; Forman. 4.43

(-) **grade**

first-grade pupil, etc.
low-grade (adj)

grader

first grader, etc.

graduate (v), to become a graduate; O.K. for *be graduated*

gram: g, spell out first time except in charts, etc.

grass roots (n)
grass-roots (adj)

(-) hand

deckhand
dockhand
farmhand
hired hand
second hand (of watch)
secondhand (goods)

(-) handed

cleanhanded
heavy-handed
left-handed
hardhanded
awkward-handed, and other
made-up combinations

handyman. But: He is a
handy man in a fight

hang-up

(-) happy

trigger-happy
slaphappy

hard (-)

hardboard
hard-boiled
hard-core (adj)
hardgoods
hardhanded
hardheaded
hard-liner
hard-nosed
hardtop

Hawaii. No abbn

Hawaiian

he. Ban on use at start
of paragraphs is abol-
ished, but make sure
people know who he is

Headlines   60
What to cap, 4.76
Use of figures, 6.6   84

head-on (adj, adv) as in
"a head-on crash" or
"the candidates met head-on"

headquarters, pl but often
with sing v, as "head-
quarters is in St. Louis"

heart (-)

heartache
heartbreak
heartburn
heart failure
heart-free
heartfelt
heartsick
heartthrob
heartwarming

(-) hearted

bighearted
heavy-hearted
kindhearted
softhearted
stouthearted
warmhearted

heaven, lc

Heavenly bodies, 4.73-4.75   59

heavy-handed

hectare: ha, spell out first
time except in charts, etc.

holy orders, lc

Holy Week

home (-)

    homebody
    home brew
    home builder
    home building (n)
    home-building (adj)
    homecoming
    home economics
    home furnishings
    homegrown
    homeland
    homemade
    homemaker
    homeowner
    homeseeker
    homesite
    homestretch
    hometown

hopefully, in a hopeful
    mood. Does not mean "It
    is to be hoped"

horsepower: hp; spell out
    first time

horse racing

hot cakes

hotheaded

hot line

hour: hr., use abbn only in
    maps, charts, boxes

hourly-wage increase

housecleaning

housefurnishings

houses (of Congress), lc, 4.7,   42
    4.8

hundreds: at least 300

Hurricanes. Cap if personi-   62
    fied: Hurricane Hazel,
    the hurricane, 4.87

hydroelectric

Hyphen, 5.49-5.54   75

    en dash as sub for, in
        confusing combinations,
        5.54
    "15-to-20-year-olds,"   76
        5.51
    fractions, hyphenate   76
        when used as adjectives,
        5.53
    multiple modifiers,   2, 75, 159
    when to hyphenate, 1.4,
        5.50, 17.1

I

Idaho. No abbn. *Ida.* may   19
    be used in a tight spot
    on map, etc.

Idahoan

Il-76, Russian plane, 11.4   134

ill (-) in adj, usually
    hyphened: an ill-advised
    move; it was ill-advised

Illinois. Abbn *Ill.*

Illinoisan

impressionism

(-) in, all words hyphened

    break-in
    fly-in
    love-in
    sit-in

inaugural address, lc

Inauguration Day

Inc. Use comma before; word
    not always needed, 3.3   18

inch, —es: in., use abbn
    only in charts, boxes,
    maps

income-tax payer, but *taxpayer*

income-tax return

India ink, 4.82   62

Indiana. Abbn *Ind.*

Indianan

individual retirement account

Infectious organisms, 12.3   137
    Reference books, 12.4

Infinitive, split it when
    advantageous, 1.29   9

infra (-): combines solid
    except before cap or *a*,
    17.7   160

in-house (adj)

Initials in place of names   71
    5.28

inoculate

insignia. It's plural; if
    you don't like *insigne*,
    use *symbol, emblem, badge,*
    shoulder patch, shield or
    whatever it is

insofar

install, installment

Institute. Cap in name,   55
    4.58

(-) insurance (adj): life-
    insurance policy, auto-
    insurance rates, etc.

insure

inter (-) combines solid   160
    except before cap, 17.7

intra (-): solid except   160
    before cap or *a* or in
    confusing combination,
    17.7

intra-uterine

K

Kansas. Abbn *Kans.*

Kansan

(-) keeper

   bookkeeper
   gatekeeper
   hotelkeeper
   housekeeper
   innkeeper
   peacekeeper
   scorekeeper
   shopkeeper
   storekeeper
   timekeeper

   BUT: unfamiliar combinations should be kept separate: pig keeper, vigil keeper

Kentucky. Abbn *Ky.*

Kentuckian

Keogh Plan

KG. After company name, no comma between, 3.3   18

kidnapping

kilogram, —s, kg, spell out first time except in charts, etc.

kilometer, —s, km, spell out first time except in charts, boxes, etc.

kilopascal, measure of pressure: kPa, spell out first time except in charts, etc.

kilowatt, —s: kw, spell out first time except in charts, etc.

kilowatt-hour, —s: kwh, spell out first time except in charts, etc.

Kings, queens. Use Roman numerals for *First,* *Second,* etc. No comma between name and number

kinky, O.K. in informal passage but don't use for people

knock down (v)
knockdown (n, adj)

knockout

know-how. Unlimited use

Koran. Capitalize. Don't quote or italicize

koruna, pl korunas. Currency of Czechoslovakia

krona, pl kronor. Currency of Sweden

krona, pl kronur. Currency of Iceland

krone, pl kroner. Currency of Denmark, Norway

kudos, singular

kwacha, pl kwacha. Currency of Zambia

L

La, Le, Les

When surname stands   98
alone, repeat particle unless
individual drops; cap or
lc as in full name. 8.6
usually cap in French   102
names, 8.14

labor-saving

Laetrile

lame duck, election loser
still in office
lame-duck (adj)

latecomer

Latin. Acceptable for a
Latin American. Also:
Hispanic persons

Latin America. Mexico,
Central and South America

Latin American. A resident
of Latin America

Latin American (adj)

Latino: objectionable to persons of
Latin descent; they
prefer to be called Hispanics

Latter-day Saints and   125
Latter Day Saints, 10.7,
10.8

law. Lc even in name. But: 44
Corn Laws, GI Bill, Bill
of Rights, 4.17

law (-)

law-abiding
lawbook
lawbreaker
law court
lawgiver
lawmaker
lawman
lawsuit

layoff (n, adj)
lay off (v)

leadoff

leftover (n, adj)

left-winger

Legal advice. Staff law-   7
yers should be con-
sulted on statements
about arrests, etc.
Further counsel avail-
able when needed, 1.23

Legal citations, 5.6   77

Legion of Merit

Legislatures, state, and   43
their parts, 4.12

less. Measures volume, not
numbers: less whisky,
fewer workers

letdown (n)

letup (n)

leu, pl lei. Currency of
Rumania

lev, pl leva. Currency of
Bulgaria

liberal, conservative, as
political faiths: no
quotes, but caution, 5.42   74

life (-)

   life belt
   lifeblood
   lifeboat
   life buoy
   life cycle
   life-insurance (adj)
   lifeline
   lifelong
   life-size (adj)
   life span
   lifestyle
   lifetime
   life work

like, acceptable for *such
as*

(-) like, as suffix, solid
except in cases of tripled
l, as bell-like, or after
proper names, as
Lincoln-like

likely, adj, not adv. Do
not say, "He likely will
go"

lineup (n)

linkup (n), but link up (v)

lira, pl lire. Currency
of Italy

lira, pl liras. Currency
of Turkey

Lists, enumerations. Three   84
ways to use numbers, 6.7

liter: L, spell out first
time except in charts,
etc.

(-) lived. As suffix, hyphened: long-lived

livestock

living room

LL.D. No space between L.   17
and D. Only medical doc-
tors and dentists are
referred to as *Dr.*, 3.2

lockout

Lombardy poplar, 4.82   62

long (-)

   long-drawn-out (separated
    after noun)
   longhair
   longhaired
   longhorn
   long jump
   long-lived
   long-range
   long-run
   longsighted
   longstanding
   long term
   long-term (adj)
   longtime

make (-)

make-believe
make over (v)
make-over (n)
makeready
makeshift
make up (v)
makeup (n)
make-work

(-) maker

auto maker
boilermaker
bookmaker
carpet maker
decision maker
diemaker
dressmaker
pacemaker
peacemaker
policymaker
speechmaker
steelmaker
toolmaker
troublemaker

man-days

man-hours

manila (envelope)

man power (for physical strength)

manpower (in collective sense)

manufacturers' tax

Maps   154

March. Spell out month

mark, pl marks. Currency
of East Germany; West
Germany also has a mark,
officially the deutsche
mark but usually just the
mark

markdown (n)

marketplace

Markka, pl markkaa. Cur-
rency of Finland

markup

Maryland. Abbn *Md.*

Marylander

Mason-Dixon Line

Mass, High Mass, Low Mass.   123
Cap in abstract reference
to rite, lc in mention
of celebration. Uses of
terms, 10.3

Massachusetts. Abbn *Mass.*

Massachusetts resident,
native, etc.

mastermind

matériel, use sparingly;
material usually suffices

matrimony (lc)

May, spell out month

Mayor Jack Rackstraw of
Virginia City; the
mayor; a mayor

MDT. See **Time**

meager

meat (-)

    meat-ax
    meatball
    meat chopper
    meatcutter
    meat grinder
    meathead
    meat house
    meatpacker
    meatpacking (n, adj)
    meat wagon

Medal of Freedom (official award)

Medal of Honor (no longer Congressional)

Medal for Merit (official award)

Medals. Set names are capped, but see 4.89   63

medicaid

Medical terms, 12.0-12.6   137
Reference books, 12.4, 138, 139
12.6

medicare

member of the National (or International) Staff of *U.S. News & World Report*

member of Congress

member of Parliament

metalwork

meter: m, spell out first time except in charts, etc.

Methodists, 10.16   131

me-tooism

Metric system, 3.16   32

Metric-system conversions, 3.16, Table 2   35

metric ton: t, spell out first time except in charts, boxes, etc.

Mexican American, an American of Mexican origins

Mexican American (adj)

Mexican names, 8.25, 8.26   106

Michigan. Abbn *Mich.*

Michigander (But: Michiganian traits or Michigan traits)

mid (-)

    midair
    midafternoon
    midautumn
    midcentury
    midland
    midocean
    midrange
    midseason
    midstream
    midterm
    mid-Victorian
    midyear
    mid words usually one word

Middle. Cap in name, lc   58
   as descriptive, 4.65

middle age (n)
middle-age (adj)

middleman

Midwest, political region,   147
   states included, 14.0

MiG-25, Russian plane, 11.4   134

mil., for million, —s (charts, boxes,
   maps)

mile. No abbn

(-) mile, in combining form,
   hyphen

miles per gallon: mpg,
   spell out first time

miles per hour: mph, spell
   out first time

Military terms, titles

   abbreviate titles be-   28
      fore full name, spell
      out with surname, 3.14
   capitalization, 4.30-4.39   48
   numbers in, 6.8   85

milliliter, —s: mL, spell out
   first time except in
   charts, boxes, etc.

millimeter, —s: mm, spell out
   first time except in
   charts, boxes; also 75-mm
   gun, 7.3-mm pistol

million, billion, 6.9   85

millowner

-minded, in combining form,
   hyphen

mineowner

mine sweeper

mine worker

mini (-), combinations one
   word unless you create a
   monstrosity. Hyphen before cap

   minibike
   minibus
   minicab
   minicam
   minicar
   minié ball, (old bullet
      named after Minié)
   miniskirt
   ministate

Minister. Cap as in Finance   51
   Minister, etc., before or
   after name; but: a fi-
   nance minister, finance
   ministers of several
   countries, 4.44

Minnesota. Abbn *Minn.*

Minnesotan

minority leader, lc except   50
   before name, 4.43

minute, —s: min., use
abbn only in charts,
boxes, maps

MIRV, MIRV's, multiple
independently targeted
re-entry vehicle, —s;
use only with explana-
tion

Miss, not used except in   98
special cases, 8.5

missilemen

missilery

Mississippi. Abbn *Miss.*

Mississippian

Missouri. Abbn *Mo.*

Missourian

MIT, no periods

Mixed metaphors. Avoid,
1.5   2

mix-up

Model. Cap as in Model 3C

Mohammedan. Outmoded; use
Moslem for the religion
or a believer

Money

country by country, 7.0   91
periodicals about, 7.1   96
sums of, style, 6.10   85

money-changer, money-
changing

-monger, in combinations,
one word

monsignor, 10.15   131

Montana. Abbn *Mont.*

Montanan

Months, which and when to   25
abbreviate and how, 3.9

Monuments. Generally capped,
4.80   61

Moody's Investors Service

moon. Usually lc, but see   59
4.73-4.75

mop-up (n)

Mormons, 10.7, 10.8   125, 126

morocco (leather)

Moslem, not Mohammedan

most-favored nation (n)
most-favored-nation (adj):
most-favored-nation poli-
cy, etc.

Most Rev., limited use, 10.15   130

New Hampshirite

New Jersey. Abbn *N.J.*

New Jerseyite

New Mexico. Abbn *N.M.*

New Mexican

newsmagazine

Newspapers, names of, 5.55   76

New World

New Year's Day

New York. Abbn *N.Y.*

New Yorker

Nicknames, 5.45   75

night (-)

   nightcap
   night clothes
   nightclub
   nightdress
   night fighter
   nightgown
   night letter
   night life
   nightmare
   night owl
   nightrider
   nighttime
   night watch
   nightwear

nine and under, cardinal and ordinal, spell out

No. Cap if in quotes: She   63, 75
said "No." But: She said
no. 4.93, 5.48

Nobel Peace Prize

Nobel Prize in literature

Nobility, when to cap ti-   52
tles, 4.45

non(-), solid except before   160
cap or in confusing combinations, 17.7

   non-nuclear
   non-French
   non-community-property
   states

none, sing or pl

non-oil

north, northern. Direction,   57
lc; name, cap. 4.64

North Carolina. Abbn *N.C.*

North Carolinian

North Dakota. Abbn *N.D.*

North Dakotan

Nov. When to use, 3.9   25

nuclear-test-ban treaty

Numbered titles. Cap word as   61
in Article I, 4.81

O

Obscenity. How to handle,   5
1.14; showing omissions,
1.15

Occupations, not capped before names: electrical engineer J. W. Watson (but
First Engineer J. W. Watson,
title)

Oct. When to use, 3.9   25

off(-)

offbeat
off-Broadway
offcast
off-color
offhand
off-limits (before noun)
off limits (after noun)
off-season (adj)
off season, the
offset
offshoot
offshore
offstage
off-white
off year (n)
off-year (adj)

(-)off

blastoff
blowoff
brushoff
call-off
charge-off
checkoff
cutoff
drop-off
falloff
layoff
lead-off (adj)
leadoff (n)
liftoff (n)
lift off (v)
payoff
runoff
setoff
slide-off
standoff
takeoff
tip-off
write-off

office, cap only in name,   41
4.5

officeholder

OHG. After company name,   18
no comma between, 3.3

Ohio. No abbn

Ohioan

O.K., O.K.'d, O.K.'ing (not *okay*)

Oklahoma. Abbn *Okla.*

Oklahoman

Old World

Olympic Games, Summer Olympic Games, summer games, the
games

once again. Strictly speaking, it means "one more time" and is unnecessary if you just mean "again"

one half: two words as noun, hyphened as adjective

onetime, former

one-time, happening once

onto, to a position on: He climbed onto a table. But: The mayor held on to her office; Jones moved on to Chicago

OPEC. Organization of Petroleum Exporting Countries

Operas, names of, quote,   73
5.39

Ordinal numbers, use figures 10th and over

Oregon. Abbn *Oreg.*

Oregonian

Organizations, abbreviations   26
of. Where initials are used, as in NAACP, generally no periods. With exception of AFL-CIO, full name should be used first. FBI and NATO may be used in a tight lead, but should be explained as soon as possible. 3.10

ounce, —s: oz., abbreviate only in charts, boxes, maps

out(-): generally solid except before cap: outgrow. But: out group; out-migrant, out-migration; out-of-doors; out-of-pocket expenses, he was out of pocket (not around)

(-)out, nouns except where noted

blackout
blowout
breakout
brownout
burnout
cookout
dropout
fade-out (n, adj.)
fade out (v)
fallout
handout (n)
hangout
hideout
holdout
knockout
lockout
look out (v)
lookout (n)
pull out (v)
pullout (n)
shoot out (v)
shoot-out (n)
shutout
takeout
turnout (n)
walk out (v)
walkout (n)

over. O.K. for *more than,* as in "the price was over $5,000"

over(-): combines solid except before cap, 17.7   160

overage, too old: solid before noun but two words after, as in "he is over age"

overall, solid before word modified but two words when alone: Over all, the picture . . .

(-)over

changeover
flyover
hangover
holdover
makeover
pullover
pushover
rollover
takeover (n)
walkover (n)

owing to. Adverbial use, "He retired owing to sickness," basically incorrect but accepted reluctantly by authorities. Adjectival use, as in "a pain owing to indigestion," more justifiable

P

Pacific states, 14.0   147

Pact. Cap as part of official name, lc standing alone, 4.27   47

page. Do not cap as in page 13

pan (-), all-embracing

panchromatic
pandemic
Panhellenic
Pan-American
Pan-Hispanism
BUT NOTE: Pan American World Airways; Pan American Union

papal bull, lc

paper (-), Varies. Combinations not in dictionary usually should be two words as n, hyphenated as adj

paperback
paperbacked
paperboy
paper clip
paperhanger
papermaker
paper tiger
paper work (office type)
paperworker (a papermaker)

Paragraphing in quotes,   72
matter of choice, 5.36

Paragraphs. One-sentence   1
paragraphs can pall, 1.2

Parentheses, 5.75-5.77   79

commas or dashes better in news copy, 5.75
used for references, as in (*See chart* . . .). 5.76

where to put periods, 5.77

Paris green, 4.82   62

parliament, lc when not a   42
name, 4.10

Partial sentences may begin
   multisentence quotes, 5.37   73

particles (*de, van, von,* 97, 98, 102
   etc.): when surname stands
   alone, cap or lc as in full
   name. Cap at start of
   sentence. 8.2, 8.6, 8.14

part time (n)
part-time (adj)
part-timer

Party. Cap in name of political 46
   group: Republican Party; the
   party, 4.22. Democratic and Republican parties

Party members. Cap words   46
   denoting: Democrats, Socialists
   (if in party of that name), 4.23

Party officials, political. Lc   46
   titles except before names:
   John Jones, Republican national chairman. 4.25

passé

passenger-mile

passer-by

Passover

pasteurize

pastor, 10.5-10.16   124

pay (-)

   paycheck
   payday
   pay envelope
   payload
   payoff (n)
   pay off (v)
   payout (n)
   pay out (v)
   payroll
   pay TV
   pay-TV system

PDT. See **Time**

peacekeeper

peacekeeping

peacemaker

peacetime

penance, lc

peninsula. Lc except when   58
   part of a name: the Iberian
   Peninsula; the Italian peninsula. 4.70

Penn Central, no hyphen

Pennsylvania. Abbn *Pa.*

Pennsylvanian

pent-up (before noun)

per capita (no hyphen in adj)

pound, —s: lb., use abbn
only in charts, boxes,
maps

pounds per square inch:
psi, spell out first time

(-) power

air power
firepower
manpower (collective)
man power (like water power)
sea power

pre(-), combines solid except
before cap or *e* or to
avoid confusion. Examples:

premedical
pre-empt
pre-judicial, prior to a
hearing before a judge,
etc.
prejudicial, harmful or
causing prejudice

Precedes. Avoid indicating   9
a text or interview has
been edited, 1.30; in precedes of
datelined articles, avoid
here, 1.31

precinct. Lc: Chesterbrook   58
precinct, 4.68

Prefixes, 17.7   160

preposition at the end of
sentence: better than
an awkward phrase

Presbyterians, 10.13   128

Presidency (of all countries)

President of the U.S., other   50
nations, cap; also the Chief
Executive, the Commander in
Chief when referring to the
President, 4.43

president of a company, uni-   49
versity or organization, lc
except before name, 4.40, 4.42

President-elect of U.S.

presidential

president pro tem of the   51
Senate: lc except before
name, 4.43

press secretary to the
President

priest, 10.15   130

Prizes. Set names capped,   63
but see 4.89

pro(-), combines solid except   160
before *o* or cap or in absurdities. Note *pro-union*, 17.7

Prof. Abbreviate before full name,
spell out before surname

Profanity. What you can and   5
can't say, 1.14; showing
omissions, 1.15

Professor. Cap before name, lc 56
after and alone; exception,
4.63. Abbn before full
name, 3.13   28

Representative John Doe
(R-N.Y.); the represen-
tative; a representative

representative-at-large

Republic, cap when refer-   41
ring to the United States
or when part of a name, 4.2

Republican (or Democratic)
Party; the party

Republican (or Democratic)
national chairman, lc
except before name

Republican (or Democratic)
National Committee; the
committee

Republican (or Democratic)
national convention

Reserve, Reserves, cap for
specific military group

reservist, reservists, lc
for members of military
group

Reserve Officers' Training
Corps, ROTC

resister, one who or that
which resists

resistor, electrical device

Restrictive clauses go   66
without commas, 5.4

retailers' tax

retired

USA (Ret.)
USAF (Ret.)
USN (Ret.)

re-use

Reverend, Rev.   123

not Reverend Pelzer or
Rev. Pelzer, 10.2
in captions, 10.2
denominational uses,
10.5 ff

revolutions per minute:
rpm, spell out first
time

Rhode Island. Abbn *R.I.*

Rhode Islander

rial, pl rials. Currency
of Iran, Yemen-Sana

right, the; right wing (n)
right-wing (adj); right-
winger

right-of-way

"right to work" law

ringleader

ripoff. A standard word

S

SA. After company name,
no comma between, 3.3   18

safe (-)

    safe-conduct (n, adj)
    safecracker
    safe-deposit (adj)
    safeguard
    safekeeping

Saint, Sainte. Abbreviate   20
to St., Ste. in geograph-
ical names except for
Saint John, N.B., 3.7

salespeople

salesperson

salesroom

Samoa. No abbn

Samoan

savings and loan associa-
tion

savings bonds, U.S.

Scandinavian countries:
Norway, Sweden, Denmark;
Iceland is sometimes in-
cluded, as is Finland,
but Finland is related
by language to Estonia,
Lapland and Hungary
rather than to Scandinavia

Schedule. Cap as in
Schedule D

schilling, pl schillings.
Currency of Austria.
But: groschen, groschen

scholar. Lc as: Rhodes   56
scholar, 4.61

Scholarship. Cap in name   56
of award, lc alone, 4.61

scholasticism

School, when capped, 4.58,   58
4.59

school (-)

    school board
    schoolbook
    schoolboy
    school bus
    schoolchildren
    school funds
    schoolgirl
    schoolhouse
    schoolroom
    schoolteacher
    schoolwork

scoreboard

score card

scorekeeper

Scores. Use figures

Scotch whisky

series E savings bonds

service. Cap only in name, 4.5   41

set (-)

    set-aside (n)
    setback
    setoff
    set-to
    setup

sexual bias, how to avoid,   14
    2.5

shake (-)

    shakedown
    shakeout
    shake-up

shape-up, longshoremen's
    hiring process

sharecropper

sharpshooter

she. Do not use for coun-
    tries. Countries are *it*.
    Use for ships

sheet metal

sheik, cap before name

shipbuilder

shipowner

Ships, names of. Ital, 5.59   77
    Ships are *she*

shipyard

shoot-out

shop (-)

    shopkeeper
    shoplifter
    shop steward
    shopworn

(-) shop

    bakeshop
    barbershop
    bookshop
    harness shop
    sweatshop

short (-)

    short circuit (n)
    short-circuit (v, adj)
    shortcoming
    shortcut
    shortfall
    shorthand
    short-handed
    short-lived
    short-range
    shortsighted
    short-term (adj)

Short stories, names of,   73
    quote, 5.39

show (-)

    showdown
    showplace
    showroom

shut (-)

    shutdown (n)
    shut-in (n)
    shutout (n)

shuttlecraft

sick (-)

    sick bay
    sickbed
    sickout
    sick pay
    sickroom

(-) **sick**, usually combines
    solid: heartsick, etc.

side (-)

    sideline
    sideshow
    side step (n)
    sidestep (v)
    sidetrack

signpost

Silver Cross

silver medal in the 100-   63
    yard dash (lc), 4.89

singlehanded

sit-down

sit-in

sit-up

six-cylinder, eight cylin-
    ders, sixes, eights, V-8

Six-Day War, Arabs vs.
    Israelis, 1967

sizable

(-) **size**, in combining form,
    hyphen except with pre-
    fix that normally forms
    one word: family-size,
    oversized

-size or -sized? No final
    d when joined with a
    noun; use final *d* when
    joined with an adjective

size-up (n)

size up (v)

skid row

sky-high

skyrocket

Slang

    usefulness and limits, 16.0   155
    don't put in quotation   155
        marks unless attributed,
        16.0
    some slang words, 16.1   155

slaughterhouse

slide-off

slipup

slowdown

slow-up

small businessman

small-business investment
company

smoke screen

snapback

Social Security. Cap for   44
U.S. system; lc for the
idea, 4.14

softhearted

soft pedal (n)
soft-pedal (v)

sol, pl soles. Currency of
Peru

Solid South: Ala., Ark.,
Fla., Ga., La., Miss.,
N.C., S.C., Tenn., Tex.,
Va.

someday, an indefinite
time in the future. But:
some day in June, on some
day that I'll tell you later

someplace (adv), but: He
is moving to some place
in Arkansas

sometime, at some time not
known or specified; dis-
tinguished from some time,
meaning a certain or in-
definite period: it hap-
pened some time ago

someway

sophist

Source lines   151

Sources. Try to be more   3
specific than "experts"
or "officials," 1.7

south, southern. Direc-   57
tion, lc; name, cap. 4.64

South, the: Deep South,
Southerner, Southern
state

South, political region,   147
states included, 14.0

South Carolina. Abbn *S.C.*

South Carolinian

South Dakota. Abbn *S.D.*

South Dakotan

southern pine

Sovereigns. Use Roman numerals for *First*, *Second*,
etc. No comma between
name and number

Soviet (adj)

Soviet Russia

Soviets, governing bodies
of the U.S.S.R. or
other Communist country.
Do not use as synonym
for the people or lead-
ers of the Soviet Union

Stars, 4.75	59

state, states. Lc when 58
referring to one or
more states of the U.S.:
a state, the state; but
cap in names: State
Liquors, Inc., 4.67; New
York State, Washington
State

State and local titles. 50
Cap only before name, 4.43

state governments and their 43
agencies, 4.11, 4.12

statehood

Statehouse (specific); but
statehouses as a group

state-of-the-union message

States, the, cap *s* when referring to the United
States as a country

stateside

states' rights, lc except in
name of an organization

statewide

Statistical articles. When 87
to sub figures for spelled-
out numbers, 6.15

status quo, no italic

staunch, as a staunch
friend; but: stanch the
flow of blood

steelmaker

steelwork

Steelworkers Union

steppingstone

step-up (n, adj)

stock (-)

stockbroker
stockholder
stock market
stock-market (adj)
stockpile, stockpiling
stockroom

stopgap

stopover

(-) store

bookstore
drugstore
food store
hat store
jewelry store
shoe store

storehouse

storeroom

(-) storm

   firestorm
   hailstorm
   rainstorm
   snowstorm
   thunderstorm
   windstorm

Storms. Cap if personi-   62
   fied: Tropical Storm
   Agnes, the storm. 4.87

straitjacket

**strategic-arms-limitation
   treaty**

streamline

Street. Spell out and capitalize when part of address

streetcar

stretchout

strikebreaker

strikebreaking

Sturm und Drang. Cap *S* and   62
   D, ital, 4.83

Style. What *USN&WR* aims   1
   for, 1.0

Su-19 (Russian plane), 11.4   134

sub (-), combines solid
   except before cap or in
   Latin phrases such as
   sub judice

subcommittee

   of Congress, cap in name   42
      but lc alone, 4.9
   in name of organization,   53
      cap but lc later, 4.50
   of organization, lc, 4.51   54

submachine gun

subpoena, subpoenaing.

sucre, pl sucres. Currency
   of Ecuador

suitcase

sulfur, sulfuric

summit conference, lc, 4.57   55

sun. Usually lc, but see   59
   4.73

sun belt

super (-), combines solid
   except before cap or
   double word: super aircraft carrier (but supercarrier)

Supreme Allied Commander   52
   Europe: cap when used with
   name, in exact form, as in
   Rufus Fox, Supreme Allied
   Commander Europe; but lc
   in altered form, as in Rufus
   Fox, Allied supreme command-
   er for Europe, etc. 4.44

Supreme Court, (federal), the Court; Arkansas Supreme Court, the state supreme court, the court

Supt. Use only in series, charts, boxes, maps

surrealism

Synagogue or Temple, 10.10   127

T

Table. Cap as in Table 2

tailgate (n), one word
tailgate (v), no quotes

taillight

Taipei, not Taipeh

take-home (n, adj)

takeoff

takeout

takeover

Talmud. Don't italicize or quote the name

Tanks, 11.5   134

tap (a phone). Standard

tape recorder (n)
tape-record (v)

(-) tax (adj): income-tax rise, property-tax payment, etc.

tax-exempt income, this income is tax-exempt

tax-free bonds, these bonds are tax-free

taxpayer, but: income-tax payer

teachers' college

teen-ager

Teheran

Telegraphese. Don't leave   10
out *the, a, an*, 1.34

Temperature. 3.16   35, 87
(Table 2); 6.17

Temple or Synagogue, 10.10   127

10 and higher, cardinal and ordinal, use figures

ten, particle in names. When   98
surname stands alone, repeat particle unless individual drops; cap or lc as in full name, 8.6

Tennessee. Abbn *Tenn.*

toehold

ton, no abbn

ton-mile

top (-)

  topflight
  top-heavy
  topmost
  topsoil

tossup

toward, not towards

townhouse, a type of tall, narrow, usually attached dwelling, usually built in clusters either in the city or outside

town house, a city residence, usually so designated because owner also has a place in the country

trade-in (n)
trade in (v)

Trademarks. What they are,   141
how used, 13.0; use generic term instead in most cases, 13.1; trademarks that now are generic, 13.2; *jeep, Deepfreeze,* special cases, 13.3; sources of information, 13.4; frequently used trademarks, 13.5

trade-off (n)

trade union (n)

trade-union (adj)

trade unionism

train-mile

trans(-), combines solid except before cap, 17.7   160

transatlantic

transpacific

Transcendental Meditation, a trademark of the World Plan Executive Council

transferable

transferred

traveler's checks

travel time (n), two words

Treaty. Cap as part of offi-   47
cial name; lc alone. 4.27; Egyptian-Israeli Peace Treaty

Triestino, resident of Trieste; pl Triestini; Triestine (adj)

troublemaker

troubleshooter

truckdriver

Truman, Harry S. (period)

U

Union names. Omit the AFL-CIO designation but identify unions outside the AFL-CIO as (independent); omit possessives except in International Ladies' Garment Workers Union and in names that use -men's, as International Longshoremen's Association; use *and*, not *&*, in union names

union shop, closed shop, no quotes

United Methodist Church, 131
10.16

United Nations, organization 45
and agencies, 4.21

University. Cap in name, 55
4.58

up (-), generally solid in combination. Exceptions:

up-country
up-and-down
(also hyphen before caps)

(-) up (nouns except where noted)

backup
blowup
breakup
buildup
call-up
changeup
checkup
cleanup
close-up
cover-up
crackup

flare-up
follow-up
foul-up
hang-up
holdup
hookup
lineup
linkup
link up (v)
makeup
markup
mix-up
pent-up (adj before noun)
pent up (after noun)
pickup
pile-up
pinup
roundup
run-up
setup
shake-up
shape-up
size-up
slipup
slow-up
speedup
split-up
step-up
tie-up
tossup
turnup
walk-up
warm-up (n, adj)
warm up (v)
windup
write-up

Upper. Cap in name, lc as 58
descriptive, 4.65

upper house, lower house, do not use for houses of Congress

uptight, up tight. An uptight person is up tight

Up-to-dateness. Keep checking, 1.24 7

usable

U.S., avoid at end of sentence within paragraph. Example: He visited often in the U.S. Senate and House members returned the visits.

USN, U.S. Navy

U.S.News & World Report, italicize

USN&WR, abbn may be used occasionally; italicize

Utah. No abbn

Utahan

V

v., versus in legal citations: *Jones v. NLRB* (italicize legal citations)

value-added tax

van. When surname stands alone, repeat particle unless individual drops; cap or lc as in full name. 8.6   98

venetian blinds, 4.82   62

Venetian glass

Venetian red

Vermont. Abbn *Vt.*

Vermonter

Very Rev., limited use: 10.9, 10.15   126, 131

Veterans Day

vice (-)

vice admiral
vice chairman
vice chancellor
vice consul
vice president
viceregent
viceroy
vice squad

Vice President of a country, cap before or after name; Vice Presidency, vice-presidential. 4.43   50

vice president of a company, university, organization: cap only before name. 4.40, 4.42   49

Vilnius (not Vilna)

VIP

Virginia. Abbn *Va.*

Virginian

Virgin Islands. Abbn *V.I.* Say "residents of the Virgin Islands," etc.

Voice of America

von. When surname stands
    alone, repeat particle
    unless individual drops;
    cap or lc as in full
    name. 8.6   98

vote getter

Votes. Use figures

vs., versus (both letters
    lc even in headlines,
    except at start of a
    line of head)

vulcanize

VW, O.K. for Volkswagen after
    spelling out once

W

walkout

War. Cap in accepted   49
    names, 4.38

    Korean War
    Spanish Civil War
    Vietnam War
    World War I, the first World
      War
    World War II, the second World
      War
    World War III, the next
      world war
    a world war

war (-)

    war front
    warhead
    warmaker
    warplane
    warship
    war work

War Between the States, the
    Civil War

ward. Lc: the fourth ward,   58
    4.68

Ward's Automotive Reports,
    italicize; credit when
    Ward's figures are used

warmhearted

warm up (v)
warm-up (n, adj)

Warrant officers, abbns,   29
    3.14

Washington (state). Abbn
    Wash.

Washingtonian

watchdog

waterfront

waterpower

watershed

waterworks

Weapons, 11.0-11.12   133

Weather phenomena. Cap   62
    if personified: Hurri-
    cane Hazel, the hurri-
    cane. 4.87

Week. Cap in name of   62
  specially designated
  period, 4.84

wheatland

wheelbase

weekday

whip, party enforcer in
  Congress: lc except be-
  fore name

weekend

whiplash

Weights and measures

  figures in, 6.19   88
  metric, 3.16   32
  traditional, 3.15   32

whipsaw

well-being

whirlybird

well-to-do (n, adj)

whisky

west, western. Direction,
  lc; name, cap. 4.64   57

whistle stop (n)
whistle-stop (v, adj)

western pine

white paper, government
  report: lc unless part
  of a name

Western World

West Virginia. Abbn *W.Va.*

wholehearted

West Virginian

(-) **wide**, combines solid:

wheat belt

  citywide
  companywide
  countrywide
  industrywide

wheatgrower

  nationwide
  plantwide
  statewide

wheat-growing (adj)

  worldwide

widespread

willful, willfully

"windfall profits" tax

windup

wingspan

wingspread

wirepulling

wiretap (n, v, adj)

wiretapper

wiretapping

Wisconsin. Abbn *Wis.*

Wisconsinite

(-) **wise,** denoting way or
manner, usually combines
solid, as in lengthwise

(-) **wise,** meaning sage in a
subject, usually combines
hyphenated: penny-wise,
etc.

witch-hunt
witch-hunter
witch-hunting

Women, how to avoid
bias against, 2.5   14

Women's names, 8.5-8.26   98, 107

Mrs., Miss, Ms., 8.5
Arabs, 8.8
Portuguese, 8.17
Russian, 8.23, 8.24
Spanish-language, 8.26

won, pl won. Currency of
North and South Korea

wood pulp

Words as words. Italicize,   77
5.60

(-) **work**

book work
brightwork
busy work
framework
homework
housework
make-work, n and adj
paper work
staff work

workday

(-) **worker,** usually solid
when the term describes
a person working in a
certain material, sepa-
rate when it concerns a
person working on an
object or in a place.
But the distinction does
not always hold

auto worker
factory worker
farm worker
farm-implement worker
ironworker
metalworker
mine worker
office worker
shopworker
steelworker

workers' compensation: replaces "workmen's compensation." Use plural even if only one person involved

workers'-compensation law, suit, etc.

working man
working woman

workload

workmen's compensation: no more; it's officially "workers' compensation"

workplace

workweek

World Bank, customarily referred to by those words; officially the International Bank for Reconstruction and Development

World Community of Islam in the West, formerly Nation of Islam, 10.12   128

World Series

worldwide

worn-out (adj)

(-) worthy, usually combines solid, as in airworthy

wrack. Utterly ruin (different from *rack*, which means torture or strain)

write-off

write-up

wrongdoing

Wyoming. Abbn *Wyo.*

Wyomingite

X

x, italic and lc for unknown quantity: *x* dollars

X-ray, (n, v, adj)

Y

yak, to chat. O.K. if   157
   setting is favorable, 16.1

Yak-28, Russian plane,   134
   11.4

yard, —s: yd., use abbn
   only in charts, boxes,
   maps

(-) yard

   back yard (n)
   backyard (adj)
   barnyard
   cattle yard
   farmyard
   front yard
   hopyard
   lumberyard
   side yard

year, —s: yr., use abbn.
   only in charts, boxes,
   maps

year-end (n, adj)

year-round

Yellow Pages

yen, pl yen. Currency of
   Japan

Yes. Cap if in quotes: The   63, 75
   answer is "Yes." But: The
   answer is yes. 4.93, 5.48

yeses (pl of *yes*)

Yippie, no quotes, member
   of the Youth International
   Party

Yom Kippur War, the 1973
   fight between Arab states
   and Israel

yo-yo, not a trademark
   but a Tagalog word
   from the Philippines

Z

ZIP codes, no comma, 5.10   67

zloty, pl zlotys. Currency
   of Poland